Informative Writing

Ken Goddard

CASSELL

CASSELL

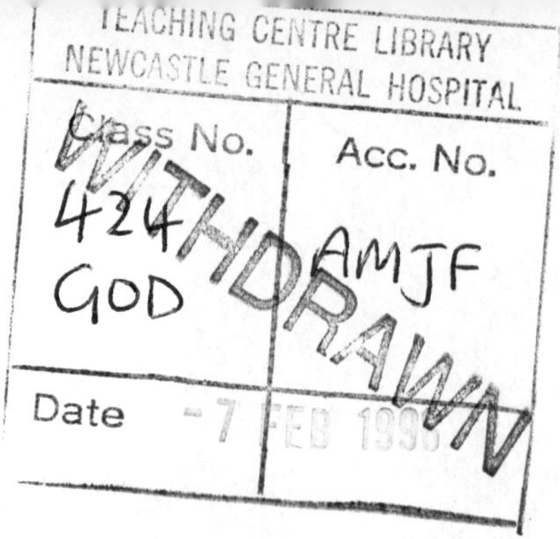

Published by Cassell

Villiers House
41-47 Strand
London WC2N 5JE

387 Park Avenue South
New York
NY 10016-8810

First published 1995

British Library Cataloguing-in-Publication Data
A catalogue record for this book is available from the British Library
ISBN 0 304 33244 5

Printed and bound in Great Britain
byThe Bath Press, Avon.

Acknowledgements

To Shirley Anderson

without whom it would have been a poorer book.

The problem with writing a book about writing is that you know it will be scrutinised with an intensity that other books don't suffer. Consequently you need a friend who can do a fearful job of criticism before others less friendly get a chance to do it. Shirley Anderson has been wonderfully up to this job. For the many drafts of this book that never twitched a publisher's eye she has been my foremost reviewer.

She has also contributed some items here and there. Thanks Shirley.

And to

Liz Hart, Dr Mike Goodland, Dr John Hill and Dr Peter Unsworth
without whom I probably wouldn't have started;
***Dr Martin Burnham, Dr Wendy Jones Nakanishi,** and Shirley Anderson again, for independently nudging me towards the definition of creative writing; **Susan Leach** for reviewing an interim draft;*
*and **Julian Streader,** recent sixth form and undergraduate survivor, for reviewing the penultimate draft.*

Contents

About this book

This book offers a methodology for informative writing. *Informative writing ranges from information on labels, through factual documents such as reports and public charters, to books such as manuals and textbooks. It's where the primary aim is to communicate facts rather than to persuade or to create an effect. Arguably it is all writing other than persuasive writing and creative writing. In all its forms it probably encompasses most of the writing that's done in the world.*

This book has been written for students but professional people should take a look too. Firstly it's for students on undergraduate Communications Studies courses or similar, for whom English is the language of study. If this description fits you, then as well as using the book as a practical guide to writing informatively, you might be asked to appraise the methodology, as an academic activity. Secondly, it's for students on any course at a similar level who have to write informative assignments in English for their coursework and for examinations. Thirdly, it could help professional people to write more informatively during the course of their work — people such as accountants, administrators, doctors, engineers and scientists. If you're a professional or a 'student on any course' as above, you'll use the book simply as a practical guide for delivering concise, precise and readable documents honed with a particular readership in mind. This is the task that the methodology aims to speed, by removing common stumbling blocks. Part 1 of the book delivers the main sequence of the methodology, Part 2 describes some techniques for special circumstances, and Part 4 consists of Appendices to support Part 1.

Part 3 explores a background agenda. It's ostensibly written for discussion by Communications Studies students in seminars but it's also reaching for the attention of educators, journalists, publishers, booksellers and librarians.

Briefly, two points. First, if you go looking in bookstores or libraries for books about writing to communicate information, you'll find them dispersed among the shelves for technical writing, business studies and English education. Second, there's a case to be made that the teaching of English for the straightforward communication of information has been neglected in favour of the more glamorous creative writing, persuasive writing and journalism. Part 3 argues that for informative writing these issues of weak identity and weak teaching are linked, and suggests remedies.

More about this book: *Informative writing and the English language*

English is a language with a large vocabulary, no gender agreements, and a flexible word order. This means it usually offers several ways to say the same thing, with great opportunities for constructive ambiguity and for exploiting shades of meaning.

For creative writers such as poets, novelists and humorists this is wonderful — English is a big toybox, a deep treasure chest. But for informative writers, the fullness and freedom of English are mixed blessings. This is because in informative writing there will usually be just one or two versions of words that will work more effectively than any others. Without instruction many people tend to produce one of the less effective versions, because the forgiving nature of English tolerates — sometimes almost invites — less effective versions. But a less effective version will transfer less information and will sometimes mislead.

So the task in informative writing is how to come up with your best version of words for your target readership, from among all the possibilities. This is the task that the methodology of Part 1 aims to ease. Notice that I've written '...*your* best version of words for *your* target readership...'. This is because firstly, *your* best version may not be the same as somebody else's best version, even after reading this book, because one of you will probably have a more extensive writing vocabulary than the other. This book can't influence that, because your writing vocabulary is a product of your lifetime reading. Neither will your best version be just a matter of vocabulary. Many things make writing *interesting to read*, such as breadth of vision, relevance to the reader, emotional colour, humour, and much else. How much of each of these you'll be able to inject will depend upon your whole life experience. This book can't influence that either.

Secondly, the best version for one readership may not be the best for another — for instance, because one readership may already know more about the topic than another, or because one may have a wider reading vocabulary than another, or because one may prefer a more formal style than another. So if the target readership changes, the words will probably need to change too.

In summary then, this book attempts only the possible, which is to get you to produce *your* best version for *your* target readership.

Forms of informative writing

***Short pieces** of writing such as:*

Labels
Memos
Captions
Glossaries
Instructions
Database texts
Curriculum vitae
Lists and catalogues
Formal letters, faxes and e-mail
Logs and diaries to be read by others
Product specifications and descriptions
Explanatory notes on technical drawings
Leaflets, brochures, publicity flyers and newsletters.

***Documents** such as:*

Public charters
All types of reports:
  laboratory reports
  medical reports
  engineering reports
  business reports
  administrative reports
  government reports
  reports of public inquiries
  accident reports
Proposals, prospectuses, business plans and bid documents
Legal contracts and terms of agreements
Insurance and pensions policy schedules
Scripts for video or multi-media educational topics
Academic essays, dissertations, theses and research papers.
Any other factual student coursework.

***Books** such as:*

Textbooks and coursebooks
Manuals, handbooks and guides
Encyclopaedias, gazetteers and dictionaries
In fact, all books classified as non-fiction by booksellers and libraries.

Common faults in informative writing

Information written for the writer, not the reader

Information written with no objective in mind

Poorly organised information

Poorly signposted information

Unnecessary information

Missing information

Incorrect information

Misleading information

Typesize(s) too small

Too much information on each page

Mistakes in spelling, grammar and punctuation.

PART 1
Principal Techniques

About Part 1

Part 1: *Principal Techniques*, consists of three chapters, each representing a stage of the methodology:

Chapter 1: Planning

Chapter 2: Writing

Chapter 3: Revising.

In the Planning stage your objective is to produce a Document Plan; in the Writing stage it's to implement that Plan most informatively for your readership; and in the Revising stage it's to hone your text in the light of comments by reviewers who typify your target readership.

About Chapter 1

Before you start writing, this chapter describes seven activities of thinking and documenting that constitute the planning stage:

Identify your readership
Identify your objective
Identify your scope
Identify your content
Structure your content
Think about diagrams and pictures
Produce the plan.

The ***target*** of this planning stage is to produce a written plan for your document or book. This is called the *Document Plan*. It will resemble a finished contents page without page numbers but with titles of any illustrations.

Broadly, the ***method*** of arriving at the Document Plan is to:

first, decide who you want to write for (unless you've been told who), and write it down in a single statement if possible;
second, decide the overall objective of your writing: why are you doing it? what are you trying to achieve? Write it down in a single statement;
third, think about your target readers' motivations and, if necessary, adjust the statements describing your target readership or objective accordingly;
fourth, use your final statements of readership and objective to help shape what your scope and contents should be. End with a shortlist of topics for your contents;
fifth, structure your shortlist of contents;
sixth, think about illustrations, and list the ones you plan to use, if any;
seventh, draft it as the document plan.

This sequence of steps is the sequence of topics in this chapter.

Notes:

*1. **Time:** There are at least two issues that will influence how much time you spend on planning. The first is the scale of your writing assignment. Obviously a label will need less planning than a book. But less planning doesn't mean no planning. Some pharmaceutical labels can carry more than two hundred words of text and can be read by millions of people, with possibly serious results for anyone who mis-reads or misunderstands them. In these circumstances it's important to get the words right. To do this you'll need to pay attention to at least some of the issues raised in this chapter about planning, such as readership, objective, scope and content. But you'll probably be able to skip diagrams and pictures, and the document plan.*

The second issue is how much you know already. For example, for a substantial document—say, of 30 pages —where you know a lot about your readership, and where you have a clear idea of your objective, scope and contents, you should be able to work through this chapter in a couple of hours. But where you haven't thought in detail about these things you should allow up to a day. Wherever you fall between these two cases, you should quickly read through this chapter first.

***2. From identifying your readership to producing the final draft of your document or book,** the step-by-step record or log of your progress might be called the Document Log — and this is the term this book chooses for it. As an example of what this might look like, Appendix C shows a document log made up for the planning stage of this book.*

1 Identify your readership

Your aim is communication,
and the effectiveness of a communication
is measured by the quality of its reception,
not by the quality of its transmission.

First step: Decide who you *want* to write for. In a written statement summarise the things that characterise these people. Your summary should be short, usually in terms of ***occupations*** that imply levels of ***education*** and ***training*** of typical members of the readership. For example: 'professional engineers', or 'undergraduate students on humanities courses', or 'the lecturer'.

Second step: Turn to the next topic, *'Identify your objective'*. First read through it, then work through the first step to produce a statement of your objective.

Third step: Think about your target readers' motivations. Will they want to buy, obtain or read what you're planning to write? Do they need to know it? If not, what might they want or need that's related to your objective? Write down your best guesses of the answers to these questions.

Fourth step: If the answers suggest low motivation in your target readers, you should consider targeting either a different readership or a wider one — in which case return to your statement of target readership and change it accordingly.

Fifth step: When you've fixed who you should be writing for, list the following:

- the ***key characteristics*** about your target readership (typical occupations, level of education and training, and ages; also perhaps gender, marital status, income or wealth);
- their ***probable objectives*** in choosing your work;
- ***what they probably already know*** about your subject or theme.

If your target readership has been identified for you

In informative writing, it's commonplace to be *told* who you're writing for. If this is the case for your project then in the first step above simply summarise who these readers are.

Notes:

1. 'Your aim is communication and...' *Without instruction most people start writing for themselves rather than for their readers. Most of us are self-centred in this way. But when you think about it, writing informatively for yourself can only be for a private diary, or for a record of a lecture, or for a meeting at work, in order to support your own recall of events. Even a business diary should be written with a secretary in mind. In other words, in all informative writing other than these examples,* ***your aim is communication****.*

2. '...the effectiveness of a communication is measured by the quality of the reception...' *It's the reading that counts. If it's not read, or if it's read without being taken in, then usually it will have been a waste of time writing it — unless it carries statutory force like a tax form or a legal document..*

3. '...and not by the quality of the transmission'. *Fine words are ineffective if your readers haven't the background or education to understand them.*

4. The need-to-know principle: *On the previous page the third step asks: 'Do they need to know it? Framed as a test, this is a formulation of the need-to-know principle, which is central to identifying your target readership and central to planning effective informative writing. To illuminate this principle, I ask: Why are you reading this book? Almost certainly it's because you've decided you need to improve your writing skills, or because someone has decided for you.*

In other words, switching to your point of view as the writer:

People will choose your work initially on the basis of their need to know.

Also, notice that it's not me the writer who's doing the choosing:

You can identify and target readers
but you can't choose them;
they choose you.

5. The thinking behind the method: *Writing with particular readers in mind will improve the reception of your message, but even better is writing with the right readers in mind. The right readers are the ones who need to know what you have to say. They'll come to you. They'll choose either to buy your work or, if they're given it, they'll choose to read with attention and to the end. Identifying the right readers for your project is the target of this topic.*

So the 'right' readers are the ones you should be writing for, rather than the ones that initially perhaps you want to write for, and this implies a check of some sort. In brief, identifying the right readers means deciding, checking against your objective, and characterising, as follows:

Decide *on the readers you want to write for.*
Check *that they're the ones you should be writing for and, if they're not, then decide who is.*
Characterise *them in detail.*

This three-part sequence is the basis of identifying your readership.

Notes *(continued):*

6. When your target readership is diverse: *It's difficult to hold in mind an image of a diverse readership but there are ways to cope with this. Usually the best way is to **write different parts of your document or book for the different parts of your readership**, and at the beginning explain what you've done. In particular, tell the separate readerships to avoid the parts not intended for them.*

If for some reason you can't do this (for example, because it's not appropriate) other techniques are to write for the part of the target readership that's...

- *in the majority*
- *most likely to benefit (that is to say, needs it most)*
- *most likely to buy (wants it most)*
- *most likely to read (hopefully the same)*
- *most likely to lead you to produce a document or book that's the best compromise for the whole readership.*

7. Which of these tactics has been adopted to cope with the diverse readership of this book? *Target readership influences not only scope and content in planning, but also style of language in writing, and throughout a whole book it's probably impossible to come up with a style that's right for both students and, say, middle-aged professionals. From this point on, the thinking was that professional people would find a book written for students more rewarding than vice-versa. This is why this book is targeted at students but expects to attract professional people. It should attract on the strength of its content, because in this instance the perceived content for students was compatible with that for professionals. So part of the answer to the question above is that I wrote for the part of the intended readership that I estimated would lead me to produce the best compromise for the whole readership. Hopefully it's also the part of the readership that's most likely to benefit.*

8. Why identify readership before objective? *Because it's usually easy to define readership without mentioning objective, but not vice-versa. This is evidence that, perhaps surprisingly, readership is the more fundamental consideration of the two. Also, in putting 'Identify your readership' first there's a link with management theory: writing in which readers' requirements are put before the writer's objectives is more likely to be successful for the same reasons that businesses that put market requirements before internal ones are more likely to be successful.*

9. What's the difference between a readership and an audience?
A readership reads and an audience listens.

10. Finally: *Even when you've firmly identified your target readership, beware, because as soon as you start writing it's still always easier to write for yourself.*

2 Identify your objective

To document for reference	a dictionary
To specify	a technical specification
To describe	a caption
To explain, to teach	a textbook
To instruct	a manual
To provoke discussion	a discussion paper
To evaluate, to recommend	a report

First step: Perhaps bearing in mind the typical objectives listed above, ask yourself what is your objective in your own writing project. It will be more specific than those above, such as perhaps: *'To explain to somebody who has never before used a computer, how to switch it on and display a ready-to-write screen of the WonderWrite word-processing program'*. Turn your mind upside down. What is your *real* objective? When you've come to a conclusion, write it down — in a single statement, if possible, as in the example above. If you have more than one objective, write them each down.

Then return to the previous topic '*Identify your readership*' and complete the third step, in which you assess your readers' motivations.

Second step: If you have doubts about the strength of their motivations, you'll usually want to target a different or wider readership, as explained in *'Identify your readership'*, but just occasionally you might want to adjust your objective to accommodate what you think your target readership is looking for. What this amounts to is asking not 'What *is* my objective'? but 'What *should be* my objective'?

Whether it's your target readership or your objective that you adjust, such a shift right at the beginning could be crucial to the effectiveness of your document or book.

Notes:

1. The sequence of steps: *If it's difficult to understand the sequence in which to follow the steps between 'Identify your readership' and 'Identify your objective', then turn to Appendix C. There you'll find the sequence listed, as part of a list of the full sequence from 'Identify your readership' to 'The Document Plan'.*

2. 'Shift' or 'adjust', not 'change completely': *The purpose of the interplay between identifying your readership and identifying your objective is not to prompt you to abandon your original objective. You probably had good reasons for choosing it. Rather, the purpose is to offer a systematic path for adjusting, shifting, customising it in response to any perceived conflict between your initial objective and the needs of the target readership. The ultimate purpose is to ensure that your work is read, by ensuring harmony between your objective and your readership.*

3. Why people often start writing without considering their objective: *Usually because, without realising it, they're writing for themselves, which doesn't require a clear objective.*

4. Different objectives require different document structures*, formats and styles of language. But here we're talking about a possible shift in objective, not a different objective. Even so, if you do return to adjust your objective after getting as far as the Document Plan, you might need to adjust your proposals for structure.*

5. If your objective is mixed *— perhaps to describe and then to instruct — then you should say so in your statement of objective. And when you're ready to start writing you should try to address these different objectives within separated and signposted parts of your document or book, and also explain at the front of it what you've done.*

6. What would be the statement of objective for this book? *The original statement went something like:*
'To offer a general methodology for professionals preparing to undertake any informative writing'.
The revised version is:
(1) To offer a general methodology for any informative writing in English;
(2) To promote the use of the term 'informative writing' to encompass terms such as technical writing and business writing, and to replace terms such as effective writing and functional writing;
(3) To seed modules of informative writing in undergraduate courses for Communications Studies, and for similar courses, where English is the language of study;
(4) To stand as a coursebook for such modules;
(5) To stand as a study skills book for other courses.

3 Identify your scope

In the context of writing, the distinction between scope and content is a narrow one. The scope of a document or book is the span of the area covered by the contents, but there may be pockets within that span that the contents don't cover.

So in identifying scope you're interested in defining boundaries — in answering the question *'How wide and deep should I cast my net?'* The target of this topic is a statement that answers this question for your writing project.

Scope depends upon your ***readership***, your ***objective***, your ***time*** (which may mean ***cost***), and also your readers' time (how much do they have available?). Sometimes your scope will have been defined for you, and sometimes you'll know your subject, your readership and your objective so well that you'll also instinctively know what your scope should be. In either case you might want to skip to the next topic *'Identify your content'*. But if you're not absolutely certain, here's a step-by-step method of identifying what your scope should be:

First step: From your knowledge of your subject and your initial vision of what you want to say, formulate an initial statement of scope to work with.

Second step: Set this statement alongside the profile of your target readership and your statement of objective.

Third step: Ask yourself the following questions: *Is my statement of scope consistent with the profile of my target readership and with my statement of objective? What do I not want to cover? How much time have I got? How much time have they got? How short can I make it?*

Fourth step: Modify your statement of scope if necessary.

Notes:

1. The question of scope leads to the question of length *which, in an academic context, leads to the practice of specifying minimum word-counts for coursework such as essays, dissertations and theses. For creative writing this practice might be acceptable but for informative writing it discourages brevity. Someone who can say in a thousand words what others take two thousand to say should be rewarded, not penalised. So for informative writing a specified word-count will usually be unwise. If given, it should be interpreted as a rough guide rather than as a minimum to be exceeded.*

4 Identify your content

*In identifying the content you should be aiming for, there are two steps: **Brainstorming** and **Shortlisting**. In Brainstorming, below, you generate ideas for potential topics for your writing project, and in Shortlisting, overpage, you select the ones you'll actually use.*

4.1 Brainstorming

There's solo brainstorming and there's group brainstorming. Group brainstorming tends to produce more ideas but it's more trouble to organise. The technique for ***solo brainstorming*** can be summarised as:

Write down everything that comes to mind that could possibly serve as a topic.
Don't bother about style, order, importance or where to write.
Just write it down.

For ***group brainstorming***, you gather together a group of people who are already involved in the writing project or who, if not involved, know something about its subject.

Then by bouncing ideas off each other, you generate a set of ideas that again could possibly be topics for the writing project.

In group brainstorming it's best to try to set aside any ideas from any previous solo brainstorming because they may confine your thinking. The required product, by either method, is a list of topics for your contents.

Notes:

*1. **It can help** to have someone sitting in just to write the ideas down, leaving the others free to think.*

*2. **If the purpose** of the writing project is to produce the documentation for a wider project, the ideas generated must relate to the writing project, not to the wider project. This is an important distinction.*

*3. **The term 'topic':** It's time to propose a method of distinguishing clearly between the topics in this book and the topics in the document or book that you're writing. Where there's a danger of confusing the two, the nomenclature we'll use to distinguish between them is: 'topic (of this book)' and 'topic (of your project)'*

4.2 Shortlisting

The task here is to reduce the list of ideas from brainstorming to a shortlist of actual topics to feature in your project — in other words, to identify your content.

The technique is to test each topic from brainstorming with the question: *'Do they need to know this?'* The result is that...

initially you tell them what they need to know, but no more.

This probably sounds patronising, but that's not the intention. In any case your readers will thank you for the result, which will be a shorter, more focused, piece of writing, matched to their needs.

If an idea from the brainstorming exercise passes this test, it joins the shortlist.

Having said this, there are three points to note. Firstly, scope and content are closely related. Therefore, to identify content here you can also ask the questions that you asked in the previous topic (of this book) in order to identify scope there. These questions will be in addition to the need-to-know test, and so are likely to shorten your final contents list.

Secondly, if your brief allows you to write around your subject then, rather than rejecting outright the topics (of your project) that fail the need-to-know test, you can reserve them in a group mentally labelled 'Interest'. But if you decide to use these, remember that this chapter is about planning and so we're talking about whole topics here, not just paragraphs or sentences.
To include whole topics that your readers don't really need to know about is a risk. At the very least it can obscure the overall thread of your writing.

Thirdly, if you decide the risk is justified then try to present the extra information in a way that makes it clear that it's an optional extra — for example, as an Appendix, or as page(s) set out as Notes, or on a shaded background, or in a different (and usually smaller) font.

The product of this topic (of this book) should be an *unsorted* shortlist of topics (of your project). In the next two topics (of this book) you sort and sequence this list.

Notes:

1 There's a logic and a symmetry *about using the need-to-know test to identify target readership, then using it back-to-back to identify the contents for that readership.*

2 The test for content *that many people apply unconsciously in their planning (if they do any planning) and certainly in their writing is 'Would this interest my readers?' This is a very open-ended test. It lets through a lot of material that the readers don't need, and that simply fogs up the landscape for them. They then have the problem of identifying the information they do need. They're not often in a position to do this because, unlike you, they don't have the whole picture. Basically, it's your job to decide what they need to know, not theirs.*

Also, unnecessary information can bring in concepts that are unfamiliar and unexplained. This can give readers the feeling either that they've missed something, or that they haven't really mastered what's going on, or that what's going on is difficult and that, if they do try to master it, it'll take a long time.

In summary, the 'need-to-know' test produces a better informative content than the 'interest' test. But that's not to say that being interesting isn't important. It's just that, as a general rule, you should apply the 'need-to-know' test fiercely in the planning stage to resolve indecision on which topics to include, and then less fiercely in the writing stage to resolve indecision on which paragraphs or sentences to include. It's in the writing stage that being interesting should be in the forefront of your mind, not in the planning stage.

5 Structure your content

*In structuring the raw list of contents that you should now hold, there are two steps: **Sorting** and **Sequencing**.*
In Sorting you apply criteria to sub-divide your material into groups, which can end up as chapters, Parts, or even different documents.
In Sequencing you sequence the topics within these groups.

5.1 Sorting

In sorting material, the main criteria are:

- the readership it's written for
- whether they'll read it once or refer to it repeatedly
- whether the information is hierarchical or sequential.

1 The readership

First, if your readership is single-type (not diverse) then structuring by readership isn't a criteria at all. But if it *is* diverse then you'll need to make sure that readers don't waste time getting to grips with information not intended for them.

In this case the technique is to allocate the information to different sets of chapters, and to specify which chapters are for which parts of the readership (perhaps reinforced by a flow-chart of the book or document).

2 'Read once' or 'refer repeatedly'

Particularly in manuals or handbooks, introductory and tutorial information will be read once and reference information will be referred to repeatedly.

It's important to separate these two types most decisively — such as into a Part 1 and a Part 2, or even into separate documents or books.

3 Hierarchical or sequential

Most large-scale information is presented hierarchically, but in some circumstances a sequential presentation is better, such as for:

- information with a structure that's genuinely and wholly sequential — for example, with a chronological basis, such as instructions.
- information with a structure that's too complex or extensive to present, or for the average reader to take in. In this case you might have to settle for featuring just one or more sequential paths through it, as examples.

Notes:

1. 'Most large-scale information is presented hierarchically...' *Why?*
A big question. In the cult classic book 'Zen and the Art of Motorcycle Maintenance' by Robert Pirsig, on pp.78-82 and 102-105 of the edition published in the UK by Vintage, there's a thought-provoking discussion of this question.
On p.36 of the same edition Pirsig also comments perceptively on the way many technical writers see the things they've been asked to write about. Pirsig worked as a technical writer and editor before and during the time he was writing the book.

5.2 Sequencing

This is about sequencing topics but it can also stand in Chapter 2 as the first part of the topic 'Within topics, the sequence of information to aim for'.

1 Level of detail

Level of detail is fundamental to sequencing any type of information. Generally some people need to read just a summary, others need to read a summary and the main body, and others need to read a summary, the main body and the detail. If that's the nature of the need, the best thing is to satisfy it:

First the summary,
then the main body,
then the detail.

A document or book with this structure permits 'peel-off':

- upper management can peel off after the summary
- middle-management can peel off after the main body
- specialists will read the whole.

Result: Information delivered to target.

If there are chapters, this sequence should apply equally for the whole document and also within chapters.

2 Context, then the main topic, then other information

First establish the context, otherwise the main topic will flounder and so will your readers.

The 'other information' in the sub-title above will usually consist of variations, limitations, or exceptions.

When this 'other information' enhances rather than underpins understanding, it will usually sit better alongside the sequential flow rather than within it — such as in a parallel column, or a box, or on a shaded background — so offering readers the choice of reading it or not.

3 Tell them three times

Tell them what you're going to say,
then say it,
then tell them what you've said.

This corresponds to:
introduction;
main body;
summary.

This might look like overkill but it isn't, because the introduction and summary can highlight aspects not evident from the main body. Also, communicating via the printed page is difficult, even when your readers are fresh, motivated and bright. These conditions don't always hold, so telling them three times can help.

6 Think about diagrams and pictures

Illustrations carry information more effectively than text

That's a sweeping statement, but illustrations do carry certain types of information more effectively than text. The truth is that most people like looking at pictures more than they like reading text, and so most textual information will benefit from pictures or graphics alongside it.

But 'most' is not 'all' and so you'll have to judge for yourself whether you should be thinking about illustrations *(Does the content warrant illustration? In the type of document or book you're writing, is your readership used to finding illustrations? If not, would they be ready for them?)*.

If you've decided to include illustrations, before you start to write it's good practice to:
1 *decide upon your tactics*
2 *form an idea of your proposed illustrations*
3 *list them.*

It's important to compile your list of illustrations before you write because, if you write first and think about illustrations afterwards, you risk having to scrap some of your text if you subsequently find that the illustrations can carry the information better.

For this topic then, the product should be a list of the titles of the illustrations you propose to use, stating approximate sizes and whether line drawings or photographs.

Notes:

1. Extremes are often instructive: *Some types of information can only be carried in pictures and other types can only be carried in text. For example, you can make a diagram or picture the centrepiece of each page and perhaps add text as a sort of extended caption. But in informative writing only educational books for young children and instructional leaflets for consumer purchases adopt this approach, each for their special reasons. Conversely you can omit illustrations altogether, but informative text without diagrams or pictures is usually unattractive to readers and hard-going. Dictionaries get away with it because nobody reads them narratively. Some business reports or technical reports get away with it too — either because they wouldn't benefit from illustration, or because the writer didn't appreciate the benefits of illustrations, or even because of convention.*

2. Why aren't there any illustrations in this book? *Because it's about writing itself and, in writing, words can be seen as falling upon one another, second by second, to create an image in the head of the reader. The idea of trying to use illustrations — images — to explain the nature and practice of writing seemed like a move against the arrow of time. In other words, to the question: 'Does this book warrant illustration?' the answer from within was 'No'. The feeling was that this was one type of book in which information would not be carried more effectively by pictures than by words.*

There are two incidental points to mention here. A disadvantage of the one-topic-per-page format is that it limits page space, and you can find that you need all the space for words. In compensation, the same format with liberal use of 'white space' on the page enhances readability even without illustrations, compared with a more conventional format.

7 Produce the plan

The final step in the planning process is the key one: producing a written plan for the document or book.

From your raw contents list (that is, the shortlist of topics that you should have produced in the course of this chapter) the procedure is:

1 *Take your shortlist*

2 *Apply the advice and rules for structuring the information*

3 *Decide which illustrations to use, if any*

4 *Produce your plan.*

You might call this a writing plan, an essay plan, a document plan, or a book plan. Whatever the name, it should specify the following:

a title

the hierarchy and sequence of topics, probably by chapters and sub-topics

the location of illustrations

particularly for commissioned assignments, an estimate of total number of pages.

For most forms of writing, the document plan will resemble a contents list without page numbers but with notes and titles of illustrations.

The plan will almost certainly change as you write — perhaps beyond recognition — because writing is a process of trial, error and refinement. But this doesn't matter. *The job of the plan is to get you started on a good footing and to serve as a flexible framework while you're writing.* It's there to be changed as you go.

Summary of Chapter 1

In the course of this chapter, if you've followed up the tasks that have been identified, you'll have produced the following:

A statement of your objective

A profile of your target readership

An estimate of their objectives

An estimate of how much they already know

A statement of scope

A set of ideas for topics, produced by brainstorming

A shortlist of topics.

The next step will have been to take the shortlist of topics and to apply to these the techniques for structuring information. Then incorporate the...

List of illustrations

...and produce...

The document plan.

Except for very small writing projects, you should not proceed to the Writing stage before you have produced a Document Plan.

About Chapter 2

In the Writing stage
your objective should be to ***catch and retain the readers' interest***
and to ***compose the most informative paragraphs and sentences***
for those readers and for that context.

The topics are:

Words and expressions to avoid
Within topics, the sequence of information to aim for
Within paragraphs, the types of sentences to aim for
Within paragraphs, the sequence of sentences to aim for
Within sentences, the types of words to aim for
Within sentences, the sequence of phrases to aim for
Write how you speak, then edit
Use analogies
Be surprising
Make it interesting

If this chapter appears to be about 'writing by rules', then be assured that it's not. Human discourse and the English language are too complex and too illogical to be fully prescribed by a set of rules. The techniques described in this chapter are just guides for first-try sentences. In each application they should to help you to produce a sentence that's more informative than the one you might otherwise have composed. If the sentence also reads well in its context, then use it. If it doesn't, then adjust it using your judgement. This isn't a retreat. Implementing the same techniques slavishly for every circumstance would produce monotonous writing, whereas attractive informative writing is marked by its variety. Unfortunately there are no hard and fast rules for originality and variety, and this takes us back to the point made at the end of *'More about this book'*: that this book confines itself to the possible. Firstly, it will guide you to the most informative structure for each sentence, but sometimes context or idiom will carry more force, and it's up to you to identify these circumstances and to adjust the sentence accordingly. Secondly, it's also up to you to judge where and in what measure to add the vision, humour, and emotional colour that will make a piece of writing more interesting, and that will give it your own distinctive style. This chapter points you in the right direction but how far you can go must depend upon your own capabilities.

10 Words and expressions to avoid

In place of these...	*...consider trying these...*
as, since	because
due to the fact that	because
in view of the fact that	because
is equipped with	has
is provided with	has
consists of	is, has
in conjunction with	with
with the aid of	with
in order to	to
throughout the entire	throughout
an example of this is	for example
final result	result
collect together	collect
in close proximity to	near
in spite of	despite
in the course of	during
pertaining to	about
commence, initiate	begin, start
conclude, finalise, terminate	end, finish
prior to	before
subsequent to	after
in many cases	often
in the majority of instances	mostly, usually, generally
a number of	some
numerous	many
assist	help
attempt, endeavour	try
allow, enable, permit	let
demonstrate, illustrate, indicate	show
facilitate	simplify, ease, make easier
require	need
utilise	use

In general:

Prefer ***short words*** to long words
Prefer ***familiar words*** to unfamiliar words
Prefer ***accurate terms*** to vague terms
Prefer ***concise phrasing*** to wordy phrasing
Avoid adjectives unless they add important information
Avoid jargon unless it's shorthand between experts.

In summary: ***Be direct.***

Notes:

1. On the previous page, *at the head of the twin columns, notice the words: 'In place of these...* ***consider trying*** *these'. So the suggested replacements aren't prescriptions that will always work better. For example, the expression 'consists of' is often just right for the context, but just sometimes you can replace it with 'is' or 'has', to better effect.*

Overall, the way to use this topic is to bear in mind its recommendations as you write but if the result reads wrongly in any way then revert to your own judgement.

2. Words and meanings. *The writer uses a word, the reader interprets it, and somewhere between lives the meaning.*

11 Within topics, the sequence of information to aim for

In Chapter 1, the sub-topic '5.2. Sequencing' can also stand as the first part of this topic.

1 Most interesting first

An effective technique, borrowed from journalism, is to copy the most interesting piece of information from the topic and to place it at the front.

This might distort the chronological (or other-logical) sequence, but a quick explanation will put this right, and the pay-off in grabbing readers' attention will usually make it worthwhile.

2 'Need-to-know'

In the remainder of your topic, you should give precedence to information that the reader needs to know.

You'll help your readers by subordinating merely interesting material to the information that your readers definitely need to know. You can do this by presenting the subordinate information either as Notes, or in a box, or on a shaded background, or in a parallel column (as here).

3 Examples before generalisations

Leading with examples usually engages readers' attention better and holds their interest better than leading with the generalisation and following with examples.

Learning from experience and example is the way we learn most things in life, from our first day. From these lessons we build our own rules, which we use to predict the outcomes of our actions and of others. Learning by experience and example is deep but laborious — too laborious for the classroom. Some teachers, lecturers and textbook writers try to shortcut this process by giving the rule first, but the effect is more like a short-circuit. A middle way is to precede the rule with a few key examples.

12 Within paragraphs, the types of sentences to aim for

In composing informative sentences there are three principles to bear in mind. To demonstrate the first one, consider the following examples:

...less effective versions are tolerated — almost invited — by the forgiving nature of English.	*...the forgiving nature of English tolerates — almost invites — less effective versions.*
Often it will be found impossible to decide your objective without deciding your target readership	*Often you'll find you can't decide your objective without deciding your target readership.*
Your approach, including your style of language and your depth of treatment among other things, will be dictated by this image.	*This image will dictate your approach, including your style of language and your depth of treatment, among other things.*
In the course of this chapter, if the tasks that have been identified have been followed up, the following will have been produced.	*In the course of this chapter, if you've followed up the tasks that have been identified, you'll have produced the following.*
Except for very small projects, the Writing stage should not be attempted before a document plan has been produced.	*Except for very small projects, you should not proceed to the Writing stage before you have produced a document plan.*

The left-hand versions are in the passive form (the passive 'voice') and the right-hand versions are in the active form (the active 'voice'). Passive forms are usually less direct, have less impact, and are less informative despite generally using more words.

However, in a few situations they are appropriate, such as...
...***when you want to conceal*** who is performing the action
...***when you genuinely don't know*** who is performing the action
...***when the reader doesn't need to know*** who is performing the action
...***when you're writing about a machine or a system*** — because it often sounds odd to talk about the machine or the system doing so-and-so, and better to say that so-and-so was done.

However, these are the exceptions. In general:

Prefer the active form to the passive.

To demonstrate the second principle:

...one's writing vocabulary is a product of one's lifetime reading	*...your writing vocabulary is a product of your lifetime reading*
The writer must identify his or her readership...	*You must identify your readership...*
So in identifying scope the writer should be interested in defining limits	*So in identifying scope you should be interested in defining limits*

In each case the right hand version says the same thing in a shorter, more direct, less stuffy way. Also, in the second pair of examples, the right hand version sidesteps the gender problem of *'...his or her readership...'*, and this is a typical benefit.

So the second principle is:

Use the definite person *('I', 'we' or 'you')* ***rather than the indefinite person*** *('one', 'the reader', or 'the user').*

To demonstrate the third principle:

English is a very extensive and flexible language.	*English is a language with a large vocabulary, no gender agreements, and a flexible word order.*
You should be able to work through this chapter in a couple of hours or in a day, depending upon circumstances.	*Where you already know a lot about your readership, and where you already have a clear idea of your objective, scope and contents, you should be able to work through this chapter in a couple of hours. But where you haven't thought in detail about these things you should allow a full day.*
A document plan is an essential part of any project in informative writing	*In informative writing, except in very small projects, you should not proceed to the Writing stage before you have produced a document plan.*

The more general versions on the left hand side are shorter but they pay a price. They lack the focus on action of the more specific versions on the right hand side. They lack impact, are less informative, and verge on the misleading.

So the third principle is:

Be specific rather than general.

13 Within paragraphs, the sequence of sentences to aim for

Consider the following paragraphs:

The English language is a big toy box — a deep treasure chest — for poets, novelists, humorists and other creative writers. This is wonderful for them. It offers them great opportunities for exploiting shades of meaning and for constructive ambiguity because it usually offers several ways to say the same thing. This is because of its flexible word order, absence of gender agreements, and large vocabulary.

English is a language with a large vocabulary, no gender agreements, and a flexible word order. This means it usually offers several ways to say the same thing, with great opportunities for constructive ambiguity and for exploiting shades of meaning. For poets, novelists, humorists and other creative writers this is wonderful — English is a big toy box, a deep treasure chest.

Although many people might think the left hand version clumsy, it's not actually wrong. In the better version on the right hand side the sequence of statements is:

1. *English is a language with a large vocabulary, no gender agreements, and a flexible word order.*
2. *This means it usually offers several ways to say the same thing*
3. *with great opportunities for constructive ambiguity and for exploiting shades of meaning.*
4. *For poets, novelists, humorists and other creative writers this is wonderful — English is a big toy box, a deep treasure chest.*

Notice the part each numbered statement plays:

1 *Context*
2 *Main point*
3 *Result*
4 *Conclusion.*

The trick is to:

1. Establish the context first, as a framework into which the main point can embed itself
2. Then state the main point
3. Then state the result *(although if the context took the form of a purpose which has obviously been achieved, a statement of result will be redundant)*
4. If appropriate, end with a conclusion. *(There will often be a distinction between the result and a conclusion).*

Here are some more examples:

It's usually practicable to pursue only two of the many things about your target readership that you might research.	*Of the many things about your target readership that you might research, it's usually practicable to pursue only two.*
Choose the objective that's closest to yours, from the list above.	*From the list of objectives above, choose the one that's closest to yours.*
Sorting by readership isn't a criteria at all if your readership is single-type.	*If your readership is single-type, sorting by readership isn't a criteria at all.*

So in general in informative writing, you should sequence sentences within a paragraph so as to present the information in the following order:

First, *the* ***context, purpose, or condition***

Second, *the* ***main point or activity***

Third, *the* ***result*** (if different from the purpose)

Fourth, *any* ***conclusion***

Fifth, ***qualifications, limitations, variations, or extras.***

However, this isn't a prescription for every paragraph. In particular, if a qualification is a major one that affects the whole context, then it can precede the main point. This goes for limitations and variations too. The sequence above is simply one that should produce a good informative sentence as a first try, most of the time.

14 Within sentences, the types of words to aim for

There are five principles in this section. To illustrate the first one, consider these examples:

...to facilitate its access and use	*...to make it easier to access and use*
...if your readership is homogeneous...	*...if your readership is single-type...*

Principle:

Prefer short, familiar words to longer, less familiar ones.

Remember the homily from *'Identify your readership'*: *The effectiveness of a communication is measured by the quality of its reception, not by the quality of its transmission.* Fine-sounding words will be ineffective if the reader doesn't understand them.

Second principle, example first:

This chapter describes several activities of thinking and documenting...	*...describes seven activities of thinking and documenting...*

Principle: ***Prefer accurate words to vague ones***

There can be a problem here, in that accurate words are sometimes unfamiliar ones. If this is the case, which to choose? Your decision will depend upon your readership and the context, but by choosing the accurate unfamiliar word you might force your readers to use a dictionary, whereas if you choose the inaccurate familiar word they'll learn nothing new and might even be misled.

For the third principle, consider these sentences:

Although as you write you can decide who you would like to read your work, you can't make them read it, because that's up to them.	*As a writer you can target readers but you can't choose them; they choose you.*

Principle: ***Prefer concise phrasing to wordy phrasing.***

For the fourth principle, consider these examples:

Informative writing is a term that I hope is fairly self-explanatory	*...that I hope is self-explanatory*
You don't need to think about scope for very long before...	*...to think about scope for long before...*
The document plan will resemble a Contents list without detailed page numbers	*...without page numbers.*

Principle:
Avoid descriptive words *(adjectives, adverbs)* ***or phrases unless they add information that the reader needs to know.***

The final principle concerns jargon. Jargon is a form of shorthand and has its place. In extreme cases one word of jargon can stand for pages of detailed technical explanation. The key is the reader. If he or she is a layman you'll need to provide the extra explanation, but if they're an expert you can use jargon.

Principle: ***Avoid jargon unless you're writing for experts***

In summary of this topic:

Prefer ***short familiar words*** to longer, less familiar words
Prefer ***accurate terms*** to vague terms
Prefer ***concise phrasing*** to wordy phrasing
Avoid adjectives unless they add important information
Avoid jargon unless it's shorthand between experts.

Overall: ***Be direct.***

15 Within sentences, the sequence of phrases to aim for

Consider these versions of the same statement:

While other permutations of words will do the job less well and sometimes will even mislead, generally there will be one sentence that will convey each item of information most effectively for all these people.

For all these people, generally there will be just one sentence that will convey each item of information most effectively, while other permutations of words will do the job less well and sometimes will even mislead.

In terms of common sense the first version is back to front because it leads with supplementary information. The result is that in the first three words it talks about *'other permutations'* but you have to read right to the end of the sentence before you find what they relate to. Also, the phrase *'For all these people',* is at the end, almost as an aside, but it's the context for the whole sentence.

Reading one such sentence is imperceptibly stressful, but reading a document or book full of them is tiring.

Now let's analyse the second version:

1 *For all these people,*
2 *generally*
3 *there will be just one sentence*
4 *that will convey each item of information most effectively,*
5 *while other permutations of words*
6 *will do the job less well and sometimes will even mislead.*

Notice the type of information carried by each line:

1 *context*
2 *condition*
3,4 *main point, result*
5,6 *supplementary information.*

This is similar to the sequence advocated for sentences within paragraphs.

So if your aim is to convey information, it's common sense to...

1. lead with the context *(usually a purpose, condition, or major qualification)*
2. follow with the main point
3. then the result *(if it's the same as the purpose, you can often omit it)*
4. conclude with any supplementary information.

Another example:

Because English permits so many, most people tend to produce one of the less effective sentences, unless instructed otherwise.

Most people tend to produce one of the less effective sentences, unless instructed otherwise, because English permits so many.

Without instruction most people tend to produce one of the less effective sentences, because English permits so many.

The third version is best because:

- It sets the scene with the important **qualification-as-context:** *'Without instruction'.*
- It then follows with the **main point:** *'most people tend to produce not the most effective sentence but a less effective one'.*
- And it ends with the **supplementary:** *'because English permits so many'.*

In contrast, the first version throws up the previous problem of the stranded leading phrase, prompting the early question 'so many what'?

The second version is better than the first, but compared with the third it's disjointed (it has to employ two commas instead of one), and again it treats the important qualification as an aside. And both the first and second versions require the clumsy *'Unless instructed otherwise'* in place of the snappy *'Without instruction'.* In general the sequence to aim for is:

First, ***context, purpose, condition, or major qualification***

Second, ***main action or point***

Third, ***result or conclusion***

Fourth, ***supplementary information or subordinate qualification.***

16 Write how you speak, then edit

Consider the following sentences:

The definitions of the above terms are as follows:	*Time for definitions so we know what we're talking about:*
Most of the writing that is done in the world is informative	*...that's done in the world...*
However, writing informatively for oneself has only one legitimate application: a private diary	*But writing informatively for yourself has only...*
However, you might consider why you are reading this book. Probably you have decided you need to improve your writing skills...	*But why are you reading this book? Probably you've decided you need to improve your writing skills...*

The first versions are formal and a bit pompous; the second ones are casual, written as you might speak. Readers nowadays will usually prefer the casual style. But strangely those same readers are more likely to *write* in the first style. This quirk of behaviour seems to appear in youth or early adulthood, across many cultures. Children don't seem to suffer from it.

The write-as-you-speak style is usually more effective at transferring information because people find it easier to read and because they're more likely to keep reading to the end. Unfortunately it's not possible to leave the observation at that, for at least two reasons.

First, readers have prior expectations of the style in which they should find sentences written in a particular document or book, and it's unwise for you as a writer to disregard these expectations. If your style is too casual for your readership, for example, you'll lose credibility. This means there are writing assignments for which you should ignore the advice that follows in this topic — for instance, when writing a report for a management that you suspect could be rather conservative.

So you must identify your readers' expectations. But you'll have done that already. Your readers' expectations of style will live in the lines of the readership profile you produced in Chapter 1 in *'Identify your readership'*.

Second, even if your readership isn't conservative, lifetime habits die hard and most people find it difficult to write consistently in the style in which they speak. Usually they end up editing a first formal draft to produce a second casual draft. This is probably just as well, for two reasons. First, people often speak to humour, to impress, or to mis-inform rather than to inform, which means that what they say isn't always logical. And second, even when their intention is to inform, most people aren't in a position to check the facts of what they're saying as they say it, with the result that a write-as-you-speak version can be unintentionally incorrect or misleading.

But if you want to, *how do you write consistently in the style in which you speak?* Some people find this easy, but for others one solution is to tape record and transcribe. But of course this is unwieldy. The alternative is simply to keep pulling yourself up and correcting when you find yourself writing too formally. In the end practice will make not perfect but better. In this there are things to look out for to speed the process...

How to edit a formal style into a casual style: Comparing the examples at the top of the previous page, the specific switches in vocabulary are:

However / But, oneself / you, legitimate / proper.

So in general, where possible:

Use 'you' (second person singular) rather than 'one', 'the reader' or 'the user' (indefinite third person singulars)

Prefer colloquial, casual words and phrases to 'respectable' ones

Don't be afraid to pose questions directly

Don't be afraid to use apostrophes such as in *it's, there's, you'll, you're, isn't, doesn't* ***and*** *can't.*

Finally:

The title of this topic is 'Write how you speak, ***then edit****'. So let's assume that you're producing text that reads like you speak. The final step — '...then edit' — is to edit it according to the principles of the foregoing topics in this chapter. That is to say, edit to optimise the types and sequences of sentences, and the types of words, and the sequences of phrases.*

17 Use analogies

Trying to think of analogies is like fishing:
the resource needs to be well-stocked.

In the context of thinking up effective analogies, a well-stocked mind means a resource stocked with facts, fiction and ideas *from areas other than the one you're trying to explain.* It's important that they're from other areas because an analogy derives part of its effectiveness from contrast. But it's also effective if it's *drawn from a topic that's familiar to the reader.* So a good analogy is one that's drawn from an area other than the one you're trying to explain, and yet is familiar to your readers. A challenge.

Techniques that can help are:

a for *a little mild alcohol*
b for *a bit of brainstorming, and*
c for *calling it off (setting aside the problem and doing something else — because then the answer is more likely to materialise).*

Each can have the effect of loosening ideas.

A final caution:
A good analogy can explain but a bad one can confuse.

18 Be surprising

Telling someone to be surprising is a bit like saying 'be creative' or 'be brilliant' — not much use. Taking a risk, this topic adopts a bare-bones approach consisting of three examples corresponding weakly to three generalisations.

Examples:

Avoid using descriptive words or phrases
unless they add information that the reader needs to know.

'Sirprus-ing' :
Surprising how similar 'surpris' is backwards.

'Be surprising': redundant advice
to a three-legged dog at a lamp post.

Generalisations:

- Copy the most surprising item from the body of the text up to the front
- Be recursive
- Be humorous

And there's more...

- Juxtapose facts that are loosely related
- Present ordinary issues from extraordinary viewpoints.

Notes:

1. In case the bones are too bare, here's the flesh. *(1) In a book about writing, the statement 'Avoid using descriptive words or phrases unless they add information that the reader needs to know' is one that readers thinking about this type of writing for the first time might find the most surprising. So here it is, copied from the body of the book and placed as the first of these three examples. (2) Recursion is a word that describes a process that repeats (recurs) by feeding on its own substance, like a snake trying to eat its own body. Hence not only is it surprising (...I think, but others may not) that the word surprise is almost a palindrome (that is, it spells backward almost the same as forward), but the word also describes the sensation you get (surprise) when you realise this. (3) The surprise in store for a three-legged dog as it lifts its remaining rear leg to a lamp-post is potentially humorous. But then, you never can tell: humour's a funny thing. Perhaps it depends on how much you like dogs.*

2. It might be worth saying a bit more about humour. *As this topic probably demonstrates, nothing destroys a writer's credibility more than failed humour! For humour to succeed you have to know your readership very well. With a diverse readership it will nearly always fail. Even a very funny person with a strong sense of humour can come a cropper when delivering the humour in writing, because so much lies in body language and timing.*

3. The techniques advocated *in 'Use analogies' can also be applied to this topic.*

19 Make it interesting

Making it interesting is a mix of
relevance, logical consistency, flow, completeness,
surprise, humour, readability...

...new developments, controversy, the writer's enthusiasm,
and presentation and layout.

The secret of making a piece of writing interesting is at least partly a cocktail of the techniques described, if not displayed, so far in this book, so this topic takes the form of a round-up.

You achieve ***relevance*** by identifying readership and objective and, from these, by identifying your scope and content (Chapter 1). You achieve ***logical consistency, flow*** and ***completeness*** partly by planning the logical structure and the sequence of chapters and topics (Chapter 1), and partly by correctly sequencing sentences within paragraphs, and words within sentences (this chapter). ***Surprise*** *and* ***humour*** are difficult to prescribe and mostly up to you. In the first group above that leaves ***readability*** which comes through paying attention to writing techniques — in particular to the following:

- being direct
- writing how you speak
- varying the length of your sentences
- avoiding bland words and turgid expressions
- using analogies
- typography and layout
- diagrams and pictures.

In the second group, the first three items — *new developments, controversy* and *the writer's enthusiasm* — are beyond the influence of this book. Presentation and layout aren't though, and what this book considers minimal best practice is more or less what you see in it.

In general: *Apply the principles of Chapters 1 and 2, and put the result out for review as described in Chapter 3.*

Summary of Chapter 2

In composing paragraphs or sentences, the three main things to remember are:

1 ***Separate the 'need-to-know' from the merely interesting,*** then...

2 ***Be direct***, *in the sequence...*

3 ***Context > main point > result > any conclusion > any subsidiary information.***

These main principles are supported by a set of subordinate principles:

Prefer the active form to the passive
Use the definite person (for example, 'you'), rather than the indefinite person ('one')
Be specific rather than general
Prefer short words to longer ones
Prefer familiar words to less familiar ones
Prefer accurate words to vague ones
Prefer concise phrasing to wordy phrasing
Avoid descriptive words unless they add information the reader needs to know
Avoid jargon unless it's shorthand between experts
Instead of 'However', consider 'But'
Instead of a 'respectable' style, consider a casual style
Where appropriate, ask the reader direct questions
Where appropriate, use colloquial forms, such as in 'I've'
Where appropriate, use analogies
Vary the lengths of your sentences
Try copying the most interesting item to the front
Try placing examples before the generalisation
Try to present normal things from an abnormal viewpoint
Be humorous, in the right measure
Inject variety, in the right measure.

Absorbing these ideas so deeply that they shape your sentences *as you write* takes years of practice. Fortunately there's an indirect but quicker method of implementing them, which is to reshape your sentences *after you've written them*. This is what Chapter 3 is about.

Chapter 3
Revising

About Chapter 3

The aim of this chapter is to refine your first draft by running it through a series of checks.

The topics are:

Check readership, objective, scope and completeness
Check structure and signposting
Check sentences
Enlist reviewers
The review cycle
Summary of Chapter 3.

Experience tells that priorities, structures, viewpoints — even target readerships or objectives — can change in the course of writing and that, for instance, what you considered the reader needed to know when you were at the planning stage may no longer be the case at this stage.

So broadly the first two topics of this chapter get you to revisit the issues of the planning stage, but from your new position. The third topic, *'Check sentences'*, offers six quick checks you can do that should weed out common faults of writing style. The fourth topic, *'Enlist reviewers'*, offers guidance on how to choose the right reviewers. The fifth topic, *'The review cycle'*, covers the checks that reviewers do. Many of the reviewers' checks are the same or similar to the checks that you do yourself but, because they're done by others, weaknesses are often revealed that you can't see yourself. The reviewers will generally work through a checklist called a Review Form that you enclose with your draft. Appendix B shows an example of a two-page Review Form.

19 Check readership...

This check consists of returning to the topic *'Identify your readership'* in Chapter 1 and checking that your statement of target readership is still valid.

...objective...

Similarly, this check consists of returning to the topic *'Identify your objective'* and checking that your final statement of objective is still valid.

...scope...

In Chapter 1, the topic *'Identify your scope'* consisted of using your statements and lists from *'Identify your readership'* and *'Identify your objective'* to help you to formulate a statement of scope. Here in Chapter 3 this check for scope consists of, first, re-assessing that statement of scope in the light of any shifts in direction that have taken place, and making any changes that might be necessary; and second, against this new statement, testing each item listed in your main Contents page and in any sub-contents lists at the front of chapters.

...and completeness

Check that you haven't omitted the beginning...
- because you assume they know it
- because you think it's so obvious that they'll see it
- because you start with your thinking ahead of the real starting point.

Check that you haven't omitted the end...
- because you think it's obvious.

Finally remember to tell them where to find any other essential information.

These checks are for information content only. There are other checks that are advisable before letting go of your manuscript, but which are mostly outside the scope of this book, such as checking for ***factual accuracy***, ***grammatical correctness***, and stylistic and typographical ***consistency***.

20 Check structure...

The cascade below shows the full hierarchy of information it's possible to meet in books, reports, and other modern documentation. Your draft contents list will be a version of this cascade — but probably not a full version, unless your project is very large.

Volumes
Parts (or Sections)
chapters
sections
topics
paragraphs
sentences
words.

The check for structure consists of re-applying to your draft contents list, and to any sub-contents lists, the techniques of the topic *'Structure your content'* in Chapter 1, making changes if necessary.

...and signposting

You'll know from your own experience that to be able to digest large amounts of written information you must be able to perceive its structure (which usually means its hierarchy) before you start reading. The best tools for signposting structure are listed below. Some are really only for manuals and handbooks.

- *a contents list*
- *a preface*
- *a flow-chart of the book or document*
- *section dividers with protruding tags*
- *chapter titles and section headings (hierarchy denoted by decimal numbering, successive indenting, or typography)*
- *page titles*
- *phrases in the body text (such as 'In the next chapter...')*
- *boxes and/or tinted backgrounds*
- *introductions and summaries.*

Contents list: *For any document or book with more than one section or chapter — and most have more than that — a contents list is indispensable . If there are several chapters, each with three levels, the best way to unload the information onto the reader is to list the first two levels in the main contents list and to reveal the third level in a sub-contents list at the beginning of each chapter. This is because readers tend not to absorb three levels in one list upfront. It also saves referring back to the main contents list.*
Verdict: The key signposting tool.

Preface: *Historically the main purpose of the preface of a book has been to state the intended readership, the objective, and to summarise the scope, content and structure. However, this rule has perhaps been broken too many times over the years, with the result that nowadays readers don't know what to expect from a piece labelled a 'Preface'. When you compound this with the rather dusty and dated image of the word, it's no wonder that writers have looked for replacements such as 'About this book'. But whatever label you choose, the function of the piece that it fronts should remain the same as for a preface: to outline the readership, objective, scope, content, and structure.*
Verdict: Important, but don't call it a preface.

Flow-chart: *Worthwhile for lengthy works where there are several possible sequences in which to read the chapters, where each sequence is for a different sector of the readership.*

Section dividers *are generally appropriate only for manuals and large bound reports, and even then they usually only repay for wheelbarrow jobs of over about 500 pages (when readers see them they know they're in for a hard time). Cardboard tags get tatty but more resilient plastic ones are available.*
Verdict: Effective if you're writing a reference tome; otherwise avoid.

Chapter titles and section headings:
In respect of:
Text: Restrict to key words, as far as possible.
Typography: Use a larger typesize than at first you might be inclined to.
Position: Be inclined to centre the text across the page rather than to left-justify, even for section headings. This is because text in the centre is more likely to catch the eye and because most people find symmetry inherently attractive.
Numbering: Useful for reference works but not so much for when the document or book is to be read narratively from beginning to end.

Page titles: *When it comes to reading text that's primarily informative — rather than persuasive or creative — many readers are thought to prefer one topic per page, with a topic title at the top of each page, as in this book (see also in Chapter 5, the topic 'One topic per page'). Given this, the same advice applies to the topic titles (page titles) as to chapter titles and section headings.*

Phrases in the body text: *Here are some examples of signposting phrases: 'This chapter consists of...' ; 'This is the first of three products required in this topic...' ; 'At this point...' ; 'You'll need this list shortly'; 'The observation at the top of the previous page...'. Such phrases help the readers to perceive the map of the overall subject area that the writer holds in his or her head, and helps them to track their progress through it.*

Boxes and tinted backgrounds: *Very effective. They improve attractiveness and readability. Also, readers can see the end before they start, which improves motivation. But you'll need the technology to produce them.*

Introductions and summaries: *Important, but keep them brief. In the sequence "Tell 'em what you're going to say, then tell 'em, then tell 'em what you've said" they are the first and last.*

21 Check sentences

You refine your text by applying certain tests to it. But if you have several tests to apply, it's difficult to hold them all in your mind as you read. Your mind tends to linger on the last item that threw up a correction or an improvement, and you miss items that need improving on other grounds. The trick is to apply just a single test — or two at the most — as you read through the text, and then leave the other tests for subsequent passes. This takes longer but produces a better edit. Bearing this in mind, here is a sequence of quick checks.

First, one for sentence structure...

Does the structure present the information in the following order?
Context, main point, result, supplementary information

...and then six for style...

Where the passive form occurs, would the active be better?

Where the indefinite person occurs, would the definite be better?

Is it possible to eliminate any words?

Is it possible to be more specific?

Is it possible to replace a long word by a short one?

Is it possible to replace an unfamiliar word with a familiar one?

These six are distilled from the principles listed in *'Summary of Chapter 2'*. The reduction to these six is for practicality not desirability. Read through the others periodically and try to bear them in mind. Eventually you'll internalise them and they'll start to shape your writing without you being aware of it.

Obviously you should also correct *errors of spelling, grammar and punctuation* where you notice them. Spelling, grammar and punctuation are outside the scope of this book, apart from the comments in Chapter 7, but other books that cover these topics well and in detail are listed in the Bibliography.

22 Enlist reviewers

A reviewer is someone who comments on your work before you distribute it to the full readership or send it to a publisher. The idea is that the reviewer points out errors or room for improvement before the boss, the publisher or the readers do.

Why should a reviewer be able to do this better than you? The answer to that is simply by not being the writer. From the moment you start to think about and research your subject, you begin to put distance between yourself and your prospective readers. Certainly by the time you've produced a full first draft you'll have been too deeply immersed in your subject for too long to be able to summon an outsider's perspective. By then you're definitely not a typical reader. Because of this the reviewing process is accepted by professional writers as an essential part of the writing sequence.

The ideal reviewer is someone who fits the profile of the target reader that you produced in Chapter 1. It also helps if reviewers are intelligent, articulate, literate, and detached from you personally and emotionally. Furthermore, if the topic is specialised, they'll need to be familiar with the subject area within which the topic sits, but not necessarily with the topic itself. You can enlist a single reviewer or several, but more than three makes the review process unwieldy.

When you send your work out for review, you should enclose with it a letter of instruction, or a Review Form, such as the one shown in Appendix B.
The letter of instruction should specify the following:

Which, in the planned sequence of drafts, this one is

What aspects you would welcome comments on. These should be:
- *the target readership: is it the right one?*
- *if it is right, have you actually written for it?*
- *your declared objective: have you actually achieved it?*
- *the structure and sequence of topics: are they right? are topics missing?*
- *the approach: is it right?*
- *errors of fact or omission*
- *errors of distortion or emphasis*
- *errors of grammar, spelling or punctuation*
- *the writing style: is it brief? readable? appropriate to the readership?*

A date by which you require the return of the reviewed draft.

23 The review cycle

1. ***Put the draft out for review, with a review form***
2. ***Receive edits or comments back from the reviewers***
3. ***Incorporate these as you think fit***
4. ***Return the draft to the reviewers for final checking.***

This is the review cycle. Extensive and important pieces of work can go round several times, though the target should always be just twice. In this respect the limiting factors will be time and patience — your own and the reviewers.

Notes:

1. ***Despite any request*** *that you might insert in the letter accompanying the draft, some reviewers will still simply scribble in the margin that something's wrong without saying how or why it is. You then have to contact them to obtain the missing information or issue the whole draft for review again with the request more strongly worded. To forestall this, it can be a good idea to strengthen your original request by explaining politely that, if reviewers wish to avoid a follow-up phone call or visit, they should be specific with their comments.*

2. ***Reviewers' comments*** *will often be too general in other ways. One technique that's effective against this is to circulate a software copy on disk instead of a copy on paper, and to specify that reviewers should replace any incorrect or misleading text by the exact text they would prefer to see. It's possible to employ this technique with photocopies too, but a software copy forces the technique by its very nature.*

3. ***No matter how much you've already revised a draft,*** *it's always possible to revise it more, so at some point you just have to call a stop. You should decide this point in advance.*

4. ***Finally, always take reviewers' comments seriously,*** *unless something happens to change your mind. Remember their advantage: they are not the writer. Unlike you they have the perspective of a typical reader.*

5. ***An example of a review form*** *is shown in Appendix B.*

Summary of Chapter 3

The aim of this chapter has been to refine your first draft.
In this process there are five steps:

1. Enlist your reviewer(s)
2. Refine your first draft by reviewing and improving it yourself
3. Issue the draft to the reviewer(s) for edits and comments, with a review form
4. Check the edits and incorporate the comments
5. Return the draft to the reviewer(s) for final checking.

For substantial documents you might have to perform the cycle more than once.

In enlisting reviewers you should look for people who fit the profile of the target reader. If you appoint reviewer(s) who don't have the perspective of the target readership you risk acting on opinions that might lead you to make changes that could make the document or book *less* effective.

In refining your own text there is one principle and six tests that you might apply in successive passes through the draft. Behind these stand the principles set out in 'Summary of Chapter 2', and also all of Strunk and White's 'Elementary principles of composition' set out in Appendix A.

In issuing the draft to reviewers you can either issue a hardcopy or a software copy on disk. Concentrate the minds of your reviewers by asking them to replace the words they object to with the exact words they would prefer. This works best with a software copy because of the ease of editing. If you have more than one reviewer you have the choice of circulating one copy or of issuing a copy to each reviewer. Each method has its pros and cons. For example, circulating one copy permits each reviewer to build upon the comments of the others, and it also means that at the end you have all the comments on one copy. But it's not the method that's normally adopted because of the time it can take for the review copy to complete the circuit.
The usual method is to issue separate copies. This is quicker, but it has the drawback that it leaves you with a pile of marked up drafts to cope with at the end of the process, many of which will feature the same remarks.

Finally, include a review form. This ensures that reviewers check for everything that they should do, and that their returns are mutually comparable.

PART 2
Special Techniques

About Part 2

Rather than a continuation of the methodology, Part 2 is more like an annexe. It consists of two chapters:

Chapter 4: Instructions

Chapter 5: Special formats.

The title of Part 2 is *Special Techniques,* and what's special about the techniques for instructions is that instructions are a special case of informative writing.
What's special about the formats is their visual appearance on the page and the tasks for which they're suited. The link is that instructions, methodologies and tutorial texts are often the tasks for which these special formats are best suited.

Chapter 4
Instructions

About Chapter 4

Whether you're filling in a form, putting up a shed, or operating complex equipment, you'll probably agree that clear instructions are important. Otherwise, at best there's aggravation caused and time wasted, and at worst you can lose an eye, a limb or even your life.

Nevertheless, it's clear from everyday experience that many people who write instructions are unaware of the basic rules. So, although it's simple stuff, apparently it still needs to be said. This chapter about instructions consists of three topics:

Sentence structure and style

Title, typography and numbering

Testing.

The first two of these highlight the aspects of writing instructions that mostly don't apply to other types of informative writing. The last one, *'Testing'*, is the counterpart of Chapter 3, *'Reviewing'* — that is to say, it describes the checks you need to make in order to ensure you've got the information right.

24 Sentence structure and style

Avoid:

1. *Examine your statements and lists from previous topics and, from these, formulate a statement of scope.*

Better:

1. *Examine your statements and lists from previous topics.*
2. *From these, formulate a statement of scope.*

Rule: ***One instruction per sentence***

Avoid:

Choose the objective that's closest to yours from the list above

Better:

From the list of objectives above, choose the one that's closest to yours

Rule: ***First the context, then the action***

Avoid:

Set up a file (a paper one), place this list as the first record in the file, and then store the file with the main document as it develops.

Better:

Set up a file (a paper one),
place this list as the first record in the file,
and then store the file with the main document as it develops.

Rule: Where you want to avoid a numbered list,
consider line-parsing (see 'Line-parsing' in Chapter 5)

Other things to avoid...

The 'should' construction: Example...

1. *You should examine your statements and lists..*
2. *From these you should....*

Rule: ***In lists, always use the imperative style*** (as in *'Examine your statements and lists...'*)

The 'having' construction: Example...
'Having switched on the device...' or 'After having switched on the device...'. This construction subordinates the first phrase in an off-hand way that will leave many readers with a feeling of uncertainty.

25 Title, typography and numbering

Title

As examples of the way the title of this topic might have been worded, avoid these:

The style of titling, typography and numbering of instructions

Title, typography and style of numbering

Style of numbering, typography and titling

The title of a list of instructions should:

- ***attract attention***
- ***be as brief as possible***
- ***be clear, not ambiguous***
- ***yet encapsulate the substance of the message.***

Typography

Avoid these styles:

1. Take your Shortlist
2. Structure and Sequence it
3. Decide where to Place your Illustrations
4. Produce your Plan.

1. TAKE YOUR SHORTLIST
2. STRUCTURE AND SEQUENCE IT
3. DECIDE WHERE TO PLACE YOUR ILLUSTRATIONS

1. Take your shortlist
2. Structure and sequence it
3. Decide where to place your illustrations

First, don't capitalise letters spuriously. It diverts attention from the message, and in any case there's no reason for it, no advantage.

Second, don't set a whole list of instructions in capital letters — for two reasons. First, you then throw away the opportunity to make important phrases stand out in capitals. Second, lower case characters are easier on the eye and easier to read quickly.

Third, choose a font and typesize that fill the available space readably. Here, if the third example was in Arial 10pt like the others, instead of in Courier 10pt, it would be fine.

Numbering

First, straightforward Arabic numerals (1,2,3...) are best. There's no virtue in using (i),(ii),(iii)... or (a),(b),(c)...or I,II,III,IV...unless you need two or more levels of instructions. Second, a long list of instructions often falls naturally into stages. If so, mark the start of each stage with a sub-heading but continue the numbering throughout.

26 Testing

Testing (that is, trying out) instructions against their intended tasks is essential. One thing you can be sure of is that you'll find shortcomings of one sort or another. As a procedure, it's analogous to Reviewing. Consequently, two topics from Chapter 3 are worth re-reading here: 'Checking objective, scope and completeness', and 'Enlisting reviewers'. Regard them as part of this topic, and read them first.

Checks

Check that you haven't omitted parts...

because you've said what to do *'if'* but not what to do *'if not'*
because you've said what to do on getting the expected result, but not what to do on getting an unexpected result, or what to do after a mistake or an accident
because you've told them to check a process, when what you mean is: *'check and, if necessary, take remedial action'*. If this is the case you'll also have omitted the range of normal readings, measurements, or other activities outside of which remedial action becomes necessary. And of course you'll also have omitted what remedial action to take.

General advice

Best, get a potential user to do the testing

Failing that, get a person who typifies a potential user.

Failing that, put the instructions aside, do something else, and then return and test them yourself

To whoever will be doing the testing: Before you start, get a pencil and paper to note down misleading or omitted steps as you come upon them. Trying to remember them later is a gamble.

Finally, whoever did the testing, it's best if you (the writer) draft the final version of the instructions yourself.

Summary of Chapter 4

The only sure way to write instructions is to perform the tasks yourself, writing down in detail every action you make — or better, getting someone else to write them down. If the process is complex, draw a flowchart — both for your own clarification and also perhaps to augment the instructions.

If it's not possible to perform the tasks yourself then, for a sequence of lengthy and fairly complex instructions, ***a good overall approach is:***

1. *Visualise the process and write down a sequence of instructions. But don't aim to get it right first time: just write down all the steps you can think of.*

2. *Then improve the sequence.*

3. *Then, if you've got the time, set the task aside but keep the list handy and add to it over the next day or two as things occur to you.*

4. *Then get a potential user to test the instructions against the actual task.*

When should instructions be presented as a list? A simple rule of thumb is: *when there are three or more separate actions to be performed* — although a list can sometimes look out of place, so you need to pay heed to the circumstances.

The next time you find yourself reading poor instructions don't just moan about them: do something. Write to the organisation and point out the deficiencies. If you're a graduating student, they might offer you a job.

Chapter 5
Special Formats

About Chapter 5

This chapter consists of four topics:

One topic per page

Landscape layout

Cellular layout

Line-parsing.

Each refers to a page format that's particularly effective for presenting prescriptive texts such as instructions, methodologies and tutorial texts.

27 One topic per page

A page-sized chunk of information is intermediate in size between a paragraph and a chapter, and this has advantages.

Advantages for the writer:

Fitting the information on the page can force you to write economically and to consider typography

Every page can carry a title; every page can look different

Changes in the structure of the document or book are easy to bring about because it's easy to re-order topics.

For the readers:

Many readers find that a page of information is the most they can digest at one reading, particularly if it's complex information

They can see the end of the topic before they begin, which reassures them that they're not in for a hard time

They get an impression of fast progress — which is probably justified.

Notes:

*1. **Allocating a topic or sub-topic** to a single page or page-side isn't a new idea, but it's not widely used. This is probably because in the world of writing the rules of creative writing dominate, and writers don't often examine these in the light of new criteria. For example, in creative writing the qualities of continuity and flow are important and so the idea of one topic per page has no value. But in informative writing, the qualities of structuring, delineation, and signposting are important, and so the idea does have value. One-topic-per-page can improve readability and comprehension.*

*2. **Sometimes the information is so complex** that continuity over several pages is unavoidable. But the idea of a unit of information that's intermediate between a paragraph and a chapter is a rewarding one, and one-topic-per-page is a good target to aim for, even if you can't always achieve it.*

*3. **Disadvantages:** Yes, there are some. One- topic-per-page can give the impression that all topics are of equal value, when they may not be. And it does limit the space available to you to get the core need-to-know information across.*

28 Landscape layout

Landscape layout is where the text is printed parallel to the longer axis of the page, so the page is wider than it is long. This is unusual, of course. The normal layout, where the page is longer than it is wide, is called portrait style. This page is printed in portrait.

Landscape pages can be bound at the side like most portrait pages, or at the top like some spiral-bound notebooks. With top-binding you read the book by flipping up the pages, with the bound edge at the top.

Advantages with either side-binding or top-binding:

Longer lines (these can be useful for line-parsed text; see *'Line-parsing'* in Chapter 5)

or ***wider margins*** (useful for annotations),

or space for ***multiple columns*** where perhaps there wasn't before

or space for ***sidelong illustrations***.

Further advantages with top-binding:

When opened flat, the eye reads in one sweep from the top of the first page to the bottom of the second. This is useful in ***step-by-step tutorial texts***, where continuity over long sequences is important.

An opened book in top-bound landscape layout occupies space towards the back of a desk, and there's often more available there than at each side.

Disadvantages with either type of binding:

Pages are slightly more awkward to turn

Pages and bindings are more prone to damage

Readers can be uncertain about the layout because it's unusual.

29 Cellular layout

Heading or summary	In a normal page layout, there's a hierarchy of *page, paragraph, sentence, word.* In a cellular layout there's *page, cell, sentence, word* — in other words, the paragraph is replaced by the cell. Cells can be the same size or different. And the type of information in each is up to you, although there are models that will work well and ones that won't.	*Differences: (1) Size: the largest possible paragraph will be the full page but the largest cell will be much smaller. (2) Shape: cellular text comes in 'chunks' whereas paragraphed text is usually the width of the page. (3) A paragraph relates to the one above and the one below but a cell can relate to up to four neighbours.*
Advantages	First, the smaller size of cells produces a ***shorter item-length*** which readers often find attractive. Second, the ***shorter line-length*** means that readers can take it in without shifting their eye horizontally more than once per line, which makes reading easier and quicker. Finally the ***two-dimensional*** nature of the matrix means more informational links are possible between cells than between paragraphs.	*These advantages make a cellular layout particularly suitable for step-by-step tutorials or for methodological texts, especially those with three-part sequences.*
Disadvant-ages	For the writer there are two disadvantages, and for the reader there's one. First, without at least a word-processor with a Table facility it's difficult to produce a cellular layout electronically. Second, it still takes quite a long time. Third, some readers can have trouble deciding which cell to read next.	*You can help readers to navigate the matrix by differentiating runs of text, usually typographically, as on this page. But there's still a decision to be made. In fact it often doesn't matter which way you read; across or down. On this page it's best to read across first.*

One way to make up a page like this

1. *On a blank sheet of paper, produce a list of ideas.*
2. *From this list think up the layout.*
3. *On another sheet of paper write the title you want, and stick on twelve yellow 'Post-It' stickers in a 3x4 matrix.*
4. *On the yellow stickers scribble the bones of what you want in each cell.*
5. *On the word-processor key in the title and a table of 3x4 cells.*
6. *Into each cell write the text you want.*

Across the matrix a sequence of heading/summary, main body, *and detail will usually be an effective way of structuring most inform-ation. It enables you to put the signposting in the heading (first column), the 'need-to-know' information in the main body (second column), and any extra information in the third column. Down the matrix, however, the sequence will probably depend more on the nature of the particular information than upon any general rule.*

30 Line-parsing

Consider the following definition of informative writing:

Informative writing is where the objective is to transfer information in writing from the mind of the writer to the mind of the reader, briefly and readably with minimum loss or distortion.

Now two line-parsed versions:

Informative writing is where the objective
is to transfer information in writing from the mind of the writer to the mind of the reader,
briefly and readably with minimum loss or distortion.

Informative writing
is where the objective is to transfer information in writing
from the mind of the writer to the mind of the reader,
briefly and readably with minimum loss or distortion.

'Line-parsing' a piece of text means choosing the line-endings to make a point or to emphasise a logical progression that might otherwise pass unnoticed, rather than leaving them to be determined by the page-width.

Line-parsing can be used to format any of the following types of texts:

- *lists*
- *instructions*
- *text with numbered lines*
- *screen text — for instance, tutorials or text for databases*

- *glossaries, dictionaries, gazetteers, encyclopaedias*
- *legal texts*
- *children's books*
- *TEFL (Teaching English as a Foreign Language) texts.*

In the following it can be used sparingly for particularly complex sections:
- *reports of all types*
- *academic papers and text books, particularly for maths, science and technology*
- *handbooks and manuals.*

Summary of Chapter 5

One topic per page — good for some textbooks and handbooks, and most reference manuals. Particularly good for methodologies because it emphasises the step-by-step progression.

Landscape layout — good for step-by-step tutorial texts where each instruction would occupy two lines in portrait but only one in landscape. Can be particularly good for presenting 'hands-on' instructions, because of the better continuation between alternate pages.

Cellular layout — again, good for step-by-step tutorial texts and methodologies, particularly those featuring a three-part sequence of either *'heading, main information, supporting information'* or *'screen prompt, keyboard/mouse action, screen result'*,
or similar.

Line-parsing — good for any text featuring a logical sequence.

PART 3
Informative writing and the English language

About Part 3

Part 3 is different. It's not an annexe of the methodology, and it doesn't expect to interest all the readership.
It consists of two chapters:

Chapter 6: Informative Writing: a new term

Chapter 7: The mechanics: why they matter in informative writing.

Chapter 6 explores the background agenda mentioned in *'About this book'* — that is, it draws attention to the weakness in identity and in education of writing simply to communicate information. Chapter 7, picking up on education, explains why competent spelling, grammar and punctuation are important in informative writing.

These chapters are written ostensibly for Communication Studies students to discuss in seminars. However, they're also reaching for the attention of educators at all levels, educational journalists and broadcasters, and publishers, booksellers and librarians.

Chapter 6
Informative writing: a new term

About Chapter 6

This chapter explores the background agenda introduced in 'About this book'. It concerns, of course, what this book calls informative writing.
The agenda, expanded, is:

First, to draw attention to the weak identity of this type of writing. At present it's diffused among terms such as technical writing, business writing, effective writing and functional writing.

Second, to remedy the weakness by offering 'informative writing' as an encompassing term. 'Informative writing' has the descriptive precision that 'effective writing' and 'functional writing' lack
and resounds with its opposite pole, creative writing, inviting contrast.

Third, to draw attention to the current lack of teaching.

Fourth, to see 'Informative Writing' established as a module in syllabuses wherever English is the language of study.

This agenda is most likely to engage educators at all levels, but it's also seeking the attention of journalists, broadcasters, publishers, booksellers and librarians.
However, *for practical purposes* the four topics of this chapter are addressed ostensibly to Communications Studies students, for discussion in seminars:

Informative writing in society highlights three ways in which good informative writing is a benefit to society: first, in improving safety; second, in improving efficiency; and third, in improving the public uptake of information.

Informative writing and creative writing questions why informative writing has such a low profile while creative writing is widely recognised and taught.
It suggests remedies. Some of the comments apply specifically to the UK.

Is all writing a mix of informative and creative? This topic discusses whether informative writing and creative writing are fundamental types of writing, and the only ones. This leads to a discussion of whether persuasive writing is a third fundamental or a hybrid of informative and creative.

Informative writing and journalism explores the distinctions between informative writing and journalism.

34 Informative writing in society

Safety

Cars, trains, aeroplanes, space shuttles, petrochemical refineries, pharmaceuticals. computers, software...all these products and constructs are documented and explained in informative writing. The type of informative writing we're talking about here is technical writing.

About ten years ago in the USA a passenger aeroplane crash was traced to misleading documentation. US technical writers for safety-critical applications now routinely take out insurance to cover themselves against liabilities they might incur through producing misleading or incorrect documentation. UK technical writers are being advised to follow suit.

One of the reasons why such measures have become necessary is that many modern technological developments are complex beyond the comprehension of laymen. Actually many of them are complex beyond anyone's comprehension, because experts are expert only in a particular part or aspect, and nor can the man at the top know everything.
For example, who is in detailed control of an enterprise such as, say, the design and construction of the space shuttle? The Chief Design Engineer, or someone with a similar title, will be in overall control but that's not the same as being in detailed control. Detailed control is achieved by the delegation of supervisory responsibilities down through the hierarchy of NASA management, out to sub-contractors, down through their management, and also by transfer of information between technical specialists of equal status but differing expertise. In this network of delegation, supervision, inspection, transfer and control, the effective media are speech and documentation, of which — as regards safety — documentation is the more important, whether it's on paper or on screen. If the documentation is incorrect, incomplete or misleading, the network will be weakened and, if the application is safety-critical, the seeds of disaster will have been sown.

Efficiency

In administration what is usually ultimately being administered is money, and documentation is the means by which it is recorded, regulated and checked. Administration thrives on a diet of money and documentation.

For at least ten years in Britain — and for longer in the USA — most managers of technical products and processes have recognised the dangers of assigning documentation work to untrained staff, but this recognition is only just beginning to reach managers of non-technical activities such as financial administration. Where administrative processes *are* still documented by untrained staff, most of the faults listed at the front of this book in *'Common faults in informative writing'* will be commonplace. One of the results of this will be inefficiency — potentially on a huge scale. Improving the informative writing skills of people working in administration won't eliminate such inefficiency, but it will reduce it. Where the scale is huge the scope for improvement is huge.

Public uptake of information

Public charters, conditions of employment, and the notes to tax forms are just three sorts of documents that most of us postpone reading, either forever or until we absolutely have to.

Some of that information could be useful, even vital, but these days it has a lot to compete with. Unless it's written and presented skilfully with the reader in mind, it won't get read. And in that case, unless it has legal force, it might as well have not been written. Unread literature is a waste of time and money. Informative writing skills could make the difference.

35 Informative writing and creative writing

Students do it; business people do it; scientists, medics, technologists, engineers, economists, administrators and many others do it. In fact, arguably most of the writing that's done in the world is informative writing.

Despite this, creative writing is the recognised term, with academic courses and an aura of glamour, while what this book calls informative writing has little recognition, few courses, and no glamour. How did this state of affairs develop and why has it persisted? This topic investigates some possible reasons and suggests some remedies.

First, when their attention is drawn to it, most people probably think that what this book calls 'informative writing' is simple: nothing to it, anyone can do it — because we were taught to write at school, weren't we? But the type of writing taught in schools in the past — in the UK, at least — has been mainly creative, centred on the analysis and appreciation of literature. Where writing to transfer information *has* been taught, it's been for specific purposes such as reports of geography field trips or experiments in science. For these types of assignments most teachers have tended to follow their forbears in advocating a passive and impersonal style in order to bestow a misleading veneer of objectivity. Unfortunately the passive style in English can be ambiguous and unwieldy,
and the impersonal style can be boring. In short, the whole approach is wrong.

This deficiency of appropriate teaching is one reason why people don't even recognise informative writing as an activity in its own right, with skills to be learned. To most people it's simply an unwelcome adjunct to their work and so they don't even set out to write informatively. Contrast creative writing, where those who do it are focused on it.

And then there's the diffusion of the identity of informative writing among at least four terms: *technical writing, business writing, effective writing and functional writing* — each of which falls short of representing the whole genre to advantage, in one way or another.

Incidentally, since about 1950 technical writing has had *some* recognition as a job and a set of skills. Perhaps more than the other terms it has stood for the whole of the genre in the public mind. Unfortunately it has a poor image, at least in the UK. You can test this at any social gathering by telling some people that you're a writer and others that you're a technical writer, and comparing the different responses. *Part* of the problem — again in the UK at least — is that word 'technical'.

At this point we leave behind the things that are open to influence, because the next thing that has to be acknowledged is that creative writing tends to be about people, and addresses our emotions, whereas informative writing tends to be about ideas, things, processes or techniques and addresses our reasoning.
Of these, only ideas can be as powerful and seductive as emotions and, even then, for a few people only.

Linked to this is that most people's perception is that success in creative writing brings fame and money whereas success in informative writing doesn't. In fact the situation is worse because, as suggested, most people have no perception of informative writing at all, least of all success in it.

Finally, within the UK there's the legacy of the British colonial past: a culture that valued the English language above all else for its literature and for the opportunities it afforded for delineating status. Correspondence sometimes flowered into wondrous wanderings. In Britain the remnants of this culture persist to this day. It's noticeable that Americans — who didn't have an empire to live off and had to use the English language in a much more workaday fashion — still write less pretentiously than the British.

Now for the remedies. The suggestion is that only identity and education are open to influence. So, for informative writing to raise its profile to reach parity of status with creative writing, the modest argument is that at least two things need to happen. First, publishers, booksellers, librarians, writers, journalists, broadcasters, educators and ultimately the various reading publics worldwide should consider the merits of ***recognising the term informative writing*** as the encompassing term for technical writing and business writing, and as the replacement term for effective writing and functional writing. And second, educators should consider the merits of ***introducing modules in informative writing*** throughout all levels of national secondary and tertiary education in all English-speaking countries.

36 Is all writing a mix of informative and creative?

There are other ways to put this question, such as:
Does all writing spring just from information and our imagination?
Are informative writing and creative writing the only fundamental types?
Is there a type of writing that's neither informative nor creative, nor a hybrid of the two?

To answer these questions we need definitions of informative writing and of creative writing against which to test examples. Consider these:

Informative writing is where the objective is to transfer information from the mind of the writer to the mind of the reader, briefly and readably with minimum loss or distortion.

Creative writing is where the immediate objective is ***either*** *simply to express the writer's own emotions or feelings,* ***or*** *to create characters and circumstances in order to evoke an emotional or spiritual response in readers,* ***or both****.*
In the most ambitious creative writing the ultimate objective is to explore those parts of the human experience not accessible by logic or reason.
Whichever the objective, the techniques of creative writing involve imaginatively creating, relating, juxtaposing, distorting or omitting information.

In practice most writing is weakly hybrid: that's to say, either informative with streaks of creative, or creative with traces of informative. Where the informative and the creative are more or less equally balanced — such as in journalism and biography — we could call them strong hybrids.

A hybrid of informative and creative writing is where the writer holds two objectives simultaneously: first, to transfer information to the reader; and second, to evoke an emotional or spiritual response in the reader.

Now, what types of writing might escape these definitions? For example, *beliefs and opinions?* Do they contain nothing of the creative or informative? And what of *prayers, hymns, and chants?*

Beliefs and opinions: When someone commits beliefs and opinions to paper, something is at risk — the facts or, more precisely, the evidence that can be used to prove the existence or truth of the 'facts'. In the interests of persuasion, the evidence often tends to get 'forgotten' or distorted. But our definition of informative writing specifies that facts should be transferred 'without loss or distortion'. So any opinionated writing that does omit or distort the evidence cannot qualify as entirely informative.

But then is it creative writing? In committing beliefs and opinions to paper, is the main objective to evoke an emotional or spiritual response in the reader? Well, probably not. Probably the main objective is to persuade the reader. However, this case isn't as black and white as the one above, because our definition of informative writing specifically excludes distortion whereas our definition of creative writing specifically includes it — but as just one among five attributes. Having said that, it's unlikely that the objective of any writer putting over beliefs and opinions would be to evoke an emotional or spiritual response in his or her readers, over and above the objective of persuading them. True, the writer might be attempting to evoke an emotional or spiritual response *as a means to* persuade, but that's not sufficient to satisfy our definition of creative writing, which implies that evoking the response must be the main immediate objective involving the readers. So opinionated writing that distorts the evidence probably wouldn't qualify as entirely creative, *according to our definition.*

The next question is: *Is it a hybrid, or is it a fundamentally different type from informative and creative?* Well, our definition of a hybrid is where the joint objectives are to transfer information and to evoke an emotional or spiritual response. But as we said above, the main objective of opinionated writing is to persuade. Is this hybrid or fundamental? Well, if informative writing is rooted in information and creative writing is rooted in our imagination, what is persuasive writing rooted in? Answer: beliefs and opinions. Which is where we came in above. Discuss.

Prayers, hymns and chants: The term that comes to mind to describe these works is 'inspirational'. Now if the objective of writing prayers, hymns and chants is to inspire, then that's an emotional effect, and so the writing qualifies as creative. So let's just check: *what are the objectives of these forms of writing?*
Well, the objectives of ***prayers*** are to worship, to ask for, to thank, to intercede on someone's behalf, and to comfort. Verdict: spiritual, therefore creative.
The objective of most ***hymns*** is certainly to inspire, and in any case they are religious poems set to music. Verdict: spiritual, therefore creative. The objective of ***chants*** is to carry the chanter to a state where the external world is excluded. Verdict: spiritual, therefore creative.

37 Informative writing and journalism

The aim of this topic is to argue that there's a fundamental distinction between informative writing and journalism, and to find out what it is.

Informative writing ranges from product specifications to professional journals, and journalism ranges from professional journals to the more frivolous tabloid newspapers. So we're not talking about two narrowly-defined and constant genres here. Each is a spectrum, and they probably overlap somewhere in the region of professional journals.

An obvious distinction between modern journalism and most of the forms of informative writing listed at the front of this book is that most journalism has to sell itself and most informative writing doesn't. Journalists learn to write articles that will help to sell periodicals and newspapers, whereas most informative writing sells on the back of a product, a process or an event, and is not itself the focus of any sales effort. Most non-fiction books are exceptions to this distinction.

Does this distinction conceal a more fundamental one between wants and needs? In other words, perhaps journalists respond to readers' wants whereas informative writers respond to their needs. Hence the importance of the need-to-know test in informative writing . Or perhaps journalists respond to wants *and* needs, but informative writers only to needs. Or perhaps *some* journalists respond to wants and needs, and others only to wants. Certainly some tabloid newspapers concentrate only on wants, and no longer pretend to cater for their readers' needs. Take a hypothetical example. On a day that parliament takes a decision that will shortly affect the lives of most of a tabloid newspaper's readers, the headline story is about a pop star's love-life or a dangerous dog. Wants are usually short term and obvious; needs are usually longer term and not immediately apparent.

Conclusion: Journalism isn't wholly informative. In order to sell, it must employ techniques from persuasive and creative writing. It's a hybrid, a strong hybrid.

Summary of Chapter 6

Suggestion: The teaching of English for the straightforward communication of information has been neglected in favour of the more glamorous creative writing, persuasive writing and journalism.

If this is the case, one reason for the neglect may be that there has been no single label encompassing terms such as technical writing, business writing, effective writing and functional writing. *Informative writing* is a good candidate because of its descriptive precision and the way it resounds with and invites contrast with its opposite pole, creative writing.

Another reason for the neglect may be that for the genre of informative writing there appears to have been no widely-published universal methodology written for students — at least, not in the UK. This book offers the elements of one.

Chapter 7
The mechanics: why they matter in informative writing

About Chapter 7

This chapter consists of three topics:

Why spelling matters

Why grammar matters

Why punctuation matters.

These topics have been written for teachers and lecturers to discuss with students on any course where the coursework or examinations involve writing informatively. The theme is to explain why spelling, grammar and punctuation — and by implication their teaching — are important in informative writing.

38 Why spelling matters

Up to the end of the 14th century, Latin and occasionally French were the languages of written communication and record in England. It was only in the early years of the 15th century that what was to become modern-day English began to be written down and taught, and then only by a few monks and scholars. These people guessed how to spell words from their sounds, and their guesses often differed from one another. The first development of printing in England in the 1470s by William Caxton (following John Gutenberg's original work in Germany twenty years earlier) prompted a small degree of standard-isation by feedback from the volume of words distributed. But it wasn't until after Dr Samuel Johnson published his dictionary in London in 1756 that most words began to settle down to what we now accept as their correct spellings. This mostly unguided process helped to produce the idiosyncratic spelling that's a feature of the English language today.

Why correct spelling matters generally

English is the most widely-used language in the world. Consequently across the world the functioning of indexes, dictionaries, encyclopaedias, databases and of course libraries depends upon widespread knowledge and acceptance of the correct and constant spelling of words in English.

Why it should matter to you personally

Much of English spelling is illogical, and to master it usually requires rote learning supplemented by extensive reading. Because of this, your ability to spell can reveal the style and depth of your education and reading. Certainly people silently draw conclusions about your education from your spelling.

Computer spelling checkers

In English, particularly UK English, there are scores of words that have the same pronunciation but different spelling. Some have different meanings (for example, complement/compliment, stationary/stationery), and some have the same meaning but different spellings for the noun and the verb forms (licence/license, practice/practise).

No spelling checker yet devised will identify misuse of words such as these, although there are some under development. At present you just have to know which is the correct spelling for the context. Having said this, however confident you are about your spelling it's still good practice to use a spelling-checker, to trap typographical errors.

39 Why grammar matters

Grammar matters because without a formal knowledge of grammar it becomes difficult to construct complex sentences that are not ambiguous.

The grammar of any language is a set of rules and conventions that rationalise the way the streams of words relate to each other. As we read, grammar helps us to extract meaning and, as we write, it helps us to convey meaning. But it has always been possible to read, speak and write simple sentences without knowing about grammar formally, because for every language except Esperanto the formal rules of grammar have developed *after* the vocabulary. What a formal knowledge of grammar brings is the ability to understand *complex* sentences quickly and to express *complex* ideas quickly. Without a formal knowledge of grammar it becomes difficult to construct complex sentences that are not ambiguous. In creative writing you can use such ambiguity to create an effect. But in informative writing you're often required to communicate complexity with precision, where ambiguity is always a hindrance.

Now, English is a language that has no gender agreements, that tolerates several word-orders to express the same idea, and that has a very large vocabulary — larger than any other language in the world. To rationalise strings of words English grammar relies mainly on definitions of the standard parts of speech such as nouns and verbs, rules about how to form the different tenses of verbs, and certain minimum restrictions on word-order. However, in complex sentences this still leaves room for ambiguity, which is usually resolved by context or punctuation, or both.

40 Why punctuation matters

Punctuation matters because grammar and context alone can't always resolve ambiguity, particularly where long sentences are necessary.

Punctuation is a symbolic vocabulary, a form of shorthand. Treating it as a vocabulary, take a look at these sample usages:

Mark	Name	Usage
.	full stop	*Use to mark the end of a sentence, statement or expression.*
;	semi-colon	*Use to separate independent clauses that are:* ***either** long,* ***or** contain commas,* ***or** are too closely related in meaning to be written as separate sentences.* *Use to separate phrases that already contain commas.* *Use to precede explanatory phrases introduced by words such as 'for example', 'namely', 'that is', when you want a stronger break than a comma would provide.*
:	colon	*Use to precede:* ***either** a list,* ***or** a long quotation,* ***or** a final clause (a statement) that explains or amplifies preceding matters,* ***or** a phrase or clause that's in contrast to the preceding phrase or clause.*
,	comma	The comma does too many different jobs to explain here, which is why it's easy to use incorrectly.

This table hints at the problem with punctuation. One symbol: more than one meaning. Sometimes two symbols: same meaning. No wonder people have trouble. From origins possibly in early printing in Venice in the late 15th or early 16th centuries, it seems that punctuation evolved to the point where it did the job passably well — given knowledgeable writers *and readers* — but no better, no further. As with spelling there was no single designer, and it shows.

Modern practice is to punctuate as little as possible. One way to approach it is to insert no punctuation at all until you reach the end of each paragraph, and then add just sufficient to resolve any ambiguities.

Summary of Chapter 7

Why spelling, grammar and punctuation matter in informative writing: Informative writing must be concise, unambiguous and authoritative — and yet be attractive to read. Competent spelling, grammar and punctuation help to eliminate ambiguity and retain authority.

You must know how to use the rules in order to know how to break them: With a well-educated readership, breaking the rules of grammar or punctuation can be an effective way of making a point. But only if you've already demonstrated that you know the rules back to front, otherwise your readers will assume you don't even know them front to back.
Once you've established your mastery beyond doubt, the effectiveness of your rule-breaking will depend upon the panache with which you do it.

About the Appendices

There are three appendices:

Appendix A: On 'Strunk and White'

Appendix B: A Review Form

Appendix C: A Document Log for this book.

Appendix A draws attention to a small book that first appeared at the beginning of this century, written by a Professor Strunk. It was one of the first to champion the style of concise writing.

Appendix B presents an example of a Review Form — two forms, actually — which you can use as a model for making up your own.

Appendix C is a set of forms for recording the decisions made as your document or book progresses through the planning stage, from identifying your readership to drawing up the document plan. ***To show how to fill them in, they're completed for the case of this book itself — so the contents apply only to this book.*** To these forms you can add more of your own as the document moves through the subsequent stages of writing and revising. The document log records the decisions you've taken and targets you've set yourself, helps you keep to them where you want to, and helps you to record changes where you want to. It constitutes a log or diary of the growth of the document or book to its final form. It can be useful when working to a deadline and/or a price for a client because, if any dispute arises as to which decisions were made, or which commitments given at any stage of the project, you'll have them fully documented.

Appendix A
On 'Strunk and White'

William Strunk was Professor of English at Cornell University in the USA around the time of the First World War when he wrote a book called *'The Elements of Style'* and had it printed privately. It's now in its third published edition and widely known as 'Strunk and White'. In that edition, on how to write informatively, Professor Strunk offers some 'Elementary Principles of Composition':

Choose a suitable design and hold to it
Make the paragraph the unit of composition
Use the active voice
Put statements in positive form
Use definite, specific, concrete language
Omit needless words
Avoid a succession of loose sentences
Express co-ordinate ideas in similar form
Keep related words together
In summaries, keep to one tense
Place the emphatic words of a sentence at the end.

E.B. White was one of Professor Strunk's students in 1919 and, thirty eight years later — ten years after the professor had died, he was commissioned to revise the book for college and general readers. Under a new section titled *'An Approach to Style'*, he added more principles, among which were:

Place yourself in the background
Write in a way that comes naturally
Work from a suitable design
Revise and rewrite
Do not overstate
Avoid the use of qualifiers
Do not affect a breezy manner
Use orthodox spelling
Do not explain too much
Do not construct awkward verbs
Make sure the reader knows who is speaking
Do not inject opinion
Use figures of speech sparingly
Do not take shortcuts at the cost of clarity
Avoid foreign languages
Prefer the standard to the offbeat.

Strunk and White developed each of the principles in less than a single page of text on average. The entire book is only 85 pages long and repays reading.

Appendix B
A Review Form

About Appendix B

The Review Form that constitutes the following two pages of this appendix is a model for a form that you might want to include with any writing that you distribute to reviewers for comment.

It's purpose is twofold. Firstly, to make sure that you get the answers to the questions for which you need the answers (rather than those for which you don't need the answers). Secondly, to make sure that the responses from each of your reviewers are mutually comparable so that, in the event of conflict and with three reviewers, you have a good chance of a 2-to-1 majority on each issue.

Title of Document

....

REVIEW FORM

1. Review of Content

Dear Reviewer: Thank you for agreeing to review the accompanying document for content and accuracy. Please write your ***general*** comments on this form or on a separate sheet of paper, and add your name. Please write your ***specific*** corrections and comments either on the accompanying hard copy draft or by inserting text between square brackets into the file (path / filename............................) on the diskette. For each specific correction or comment, please give the exact information you think should be there, preferably in the exact words you would like to see. This will save me troubling you with a follow-up phone call.

In your review would you please look for any of the following shortcomings...

- incorrect information
- misleading information
- omitted information
- unnecessary information

...and would you please answer the following questions:

Global issues

1. Is the stated ***readership*** consistent with the stated objective and, if so, is the language and approach appropriate?
2. Is the stated ***objective*** of the document realistic and useful and, if so, does the document achieve it?
3. Is the stated ***scope*** consistent with the readership and objective and, if so, is it met?

Content and structure

4. Within the scope covered, are there any ***omissions of content***? What are they?
5. Could the ***sequence of chapters*** be improved? If so, how?
6. Within any chapter, could the ***sequence of information*** be improved? If so, how?

It would help if you could return your review by......................... to the address / room number below. Thank you for your co-operation.

Address:
Room number:
Telephone extension:

Title of Document

....

2. Review of Style

Dear Reviewer: Thank you for agreeing to review the accompanying document for style of writing and presentation. Please write your ***general*** comments on this form or on a separate sheet of paper, and add your name. Please write your ***specific*** corrections and comments either on the accompanying hard copy draft or by inserting text between square brackets into the file (path / filename.....................) on the diskette. For each specific correction or comment, please give the exact information you think should be there, preferably in the exact words you would like to see. This will save me bothering you with a follow-up phone call.

In your review could you please answer the following questions (numbering continued from the Review of Content):

Writing

7 Is the ***level and style of language*** appropriate for the readership? If not, please say why not, and how you think general improvements could be made. Please indicate specific improvements on the hard copy draft or insert them onto the file on the accompanying diskette.
8 Are the ***spelling, grammar and punctuation*** faultless? If not, please say what you think are general faults. Please indicate any specific corrections on the hard copy draft or insert them onto the file on the accompanying diskette.

Graphics and layout

9 Is the ***graphical content*** adequate? If not, how could it be improved in general? Please indicate specific suggestions on the hard copy.
10 Could the ***page layout and typography*** be improved? If so, where and how?

Consistency

11 Are ***terminology, conventions, layout and typography*** consistent throughout the document? If not, please mark up specific corrections on the hard copy.

It would help if you could return your review by ....to the address / room number below. Thank you for your co-operation.

Address:
Room number:
Telephone extension:

Appendix C
A Document Log for this book

About Appendix C

This appendix consists of a sequence of forms called a Document Log ***that, as an example, has been completed for the case of this book itself.*** The idea is that as you conceive, plan, write and revise your document or book you fill in the forms with information. In conception and planning this information helps you set the right targets, and in writing and revision it keeps you locked onto those targets. Where you want to divert from the targets it helps you to keep a record of the diversions.

If you glance at the following pages you'll see that both the forms and their contents are word-processed, but in practice this isn't necessary. The quickest way is just to grab some sheets of A4 paper, write the title at the top of each (as you find them on the forms in this appendix), and then write in long-hand on each sheet as you come to it.

In this appendix, the forms are just for the planning stage because that's the most structured stage. In the writing and revising stages all you really need are subsequent sheets of paper on which to record notes.

The sequence in which you need the forms in the planning stage is the sequence in which they're presented in this appendix. However, there's a twist. Three of the forms are divided into two halves where the left-hand half is for a first version of the information and the right-hand half is for a possible revised version. For two of these forms you fill in the left hand side and then turn to other forms before perhaps returning to fill in the right hand side. So, to make sure you don't go adrift, over the page you'll find the complete sequence in which you should work through the *parts of* the forms.

A final point: The Document Plan arrived at in this Document Log differs from the Contents List of this book. For example, Chapters 6, 7 and 8 have no titles. This is because for most projects the Document Plan will change as the project progresses (writing is a process of trial, error and refinement). The job of the Document Plan is to get you started on a good footing and to serve as a flexible framework while you're writing.

Sequence for working through the Document Log forms

1. Readership (1) : *Statement of target readership* : First version (LH side)
2. Objective : *Statement of objective* : First version (LH side)
3. Readership (2) : *Motivation*
4. Readership (1) : *Statement of target readership* : Revised version (RH side) or: Objective : *Statement of objective* : Revised version (RH side); or both.
5. Readership (3) : *Key characteristics*
6. Readership (4) : *Readers' objectives*
7. Readership (5) : *What they probably already know*
8. Scope : *Statement of scope* : First version (LH side)
9. Scope : *Statement of scope* : Revised version (RH side)
10. Contents (1) : *Brainstorming*
11. Contents (2) : *Shortlisting*
12. Contents (3) : *Diagrams and pictures*
13. The Document Plan

Notes:

1. There's probably no better way to explain how the two-column format works than to explain the contents of the first sheet of the Document Log, the one titled 'Readership (1), Statement of target readership'. The readership I originally had in mind for this book was professional people, and this is summarised in the left hand column of that sheet. But on thinking about the likely motivation of working professional people to buy and read the completed book — thinking which is prescribed in the third step of the first topic of this book, 'Identify your readership' and recorded in the third sheet of this document log, 'Readership (2), Motivation(s)' — I decided that the best course would be to write the book for students. And in retrospect I'm very glad that I did. This revised readership is summarised in the right hand column of the first sheet, 'Readership (1)', and documented fully in the fourth sheet, 'Readership (3), Key characteristics'.

Document Log

for

..........*Informative Writing*............

Readership (1)

Statement of target readership(s)

First version	Revised version
Professional people who need to write informatively in English at work.	(1) Students at undergraduate level, on Communications Studies courses or similar, where English is the native language. (2) Students on any course at a similar level throughout the English-speaking world. (3) The scope and contents should also attract professional people who need to write informatively in English at work.

Document Log for ....Informative Writing................. 1 of 12

Objective

Statement of objective(s)

First version	Revised version
To offer a general methodology for any writing of an informative nature in English.	*(1) To offer a universal methodology for any informative writing in English.* *(2) To promote the use of the term 'informative writing' to encompass other terms such as technical writing, business writing, effective writing and functional writing.* *(3) To seed modules of informative writing in courses for Communications Studies worldwide, and in related courses.* *(4) To stand as a coursebook for such modules.* *(5) To stand as a study skills book for other courses.*

Document Log for ....Informative Writing................. 2 of 12

Readership (2)
Motivation(s)

Readership: *The initial target readership consists of professional people who need to write informatively at work.*

Motivation: *A professional person will more likely read this book because they've been told to, rather than because they've chosen to. This is because professional people rarely place their own writing skills at the top of their agenda. Their managers might be more concerned, but there will be other skills competing for training time.*

First conclusion: *The readership will probably be low in numbers and low in self-motivation.*

Options: *(1) Write for a different readership ·(2) Write for a wider readership (3) Change the objective.*

Recommendation: *Write for a wider readership.*

Justification: *The current readership isn't the wrong one: professional people will almost certainly benefit from this book. It's just that they're unlikely to buy it. Neither is the objective wrong: a methodology that guides any writing of an informative nature is possibly a new development and one that could help a lot of people. But what sort of people, besides working professionals? Answer: people aspiring and training to be working professionals — in other words, students.*

Second conclusion: *Write the book primarily for students, with professional people as an untargeted secondary readership. In practice this means writing the book with students in the forefront of your mind, in the belief that the resulting book will also be useful to professional readers.*

Document Log for ....Informative Writing................. 3 of 12

Readership (3)
Key characteristics

Occupation(s)
(1) Students at undergraduate level where English is the native language — firstly those on Communications Studies courses or similar, and secondly those on any other course where writing informatively is an implied requirement of the coursework
(2) Professional people who need to write informatively at work, such as accountants, administrators, business people, doctors, engineers, scientists, and managers of all types.

Education and training:
Students: Should be In possession of the minimum entry requirements to university.
Professionals: Minimum as above, but many will be graduates and some will have higher degrees.

Ages: *Students: 18 - 21 and older; professionals: 21 - 50 and occasionally older.*

Gender: *Male or female*

Marital status: *Any*

Income:
In the UK in 1995: Students approx £3000 per year; professionals at least £12,000 per year

Other relevant characteristics:

Document Log for ....Informative Writing................. 4 of 12

Readership (4)
Readers' objectives

For students on Communications Studies courses, or similar courses, *where this book has been adopted as a coursebook: Their objectives will be to use the book (1) to successfully complete coursework assignments based on the book (2) to help them to plan, write and revise other assignments not necessarily based on the book.*

For students on any other courses at undergraduate level, *where the book might be recommended as a useful study skills book: The objectives of these students will be to use the book to write better coursework assignments than they might otherwise do.*

For professionals: *Their objective will be to improve the effectiveness of their informative writing*

Document Log for ....Informative Writing................. 5 of 12

Readership (5)
What they probably already know

Students on Communications Studies courses, or similar courses, in the USA:
There are hundreds of courses in Communications Studies in the USA, plus reputedly 61 undergraduate courses in Technical Writing or Technical Communications. Probably most of these currently teach most of the techniques advanced in this book. Certainly the courses in Technical Writing or Technical Communications will. But what this book does is, firstly, ***it recognises*** *that these techniques apply to the communication of any information in writing, not just technical information; and secondly,* ***it builds*** *them into a universal methodology.*

Students on Communications Studies courses, or similar courses, in the UK:
Depending on at what stage of the course they've reached, they'll have learned something of the theory and practice of creative writing, persuasive writing and journalism, but little or nothing of informative writing — unless they're one of the two hundred or so students on one of the three courses available in Technical Writing or Technical Communications at HND and degree level in the UK.

Students on similar courses in Canada and Australasia:
Knowledge and awareness of the techniques of informative writing will probably lie somewhere between the cases for the USA and the UK.

Students on any other courses at a similar level:
Probably most will be unaware of the techniques — less so in the USA, more so in the UK.

Professionals everywhere:
Some will be aware of the existence of the techniques, and a few may have attended one- or two-day courses on effective writing.

Document Log for ....Informative Writing................. 6 of 12

Scope

Statement of scope

First version	*Revised version*
Include: • *Planning, style of writing, and revision* • *Special techniques to consider when writing instructions, and special formats in which to present writing of an instructional nature.* *Exclude:* • *Considerations of spelling, grammar and punctuation.*	*Include:* • *Planning, style of writing, and revision* • *Special techniques to consider when writing instructions, and special formats in which to present writing of an instructional nature.* • *Topics on the relationship between informative writing, creative writing, persuasive writing, and journalism.* • *Topics on the importance of competent spelling, grammar and punctuation in informative writing.* *Exclude:* • *Explicit instructions on spelling, grammar and punctuation.*

Contents (1)
Brainstorming

Document Log for ....Informative Writing................. 8 of 12

Contents (2)
Shortlisting

Document Log for ....Informative Writing................. 9 of 12

Contents (3)
Diagrams and pictures

Probably none

Document Log for ....Informative Writing.................. 10 of 12

The Document Plan

About this book

PART 1: PRINCIPAL TECHNIQUES

Chapter 1: Planning

About Chapter 1
Identify your objective
Identify your readership
Identify your scope
Brainstorming
Shortlisting
Structuring information
Sequencing information
Diagrams and pictures
Producing the plan
Summary of Chapter 1

Chapter 2: Writing

About Chapter 2
Words and expressions to avoid
Write how you speak
Within paragraphs, the types of sentences to use
Within paragraphs, the sequence of sentences to use
Within sentences, the types of words to use
Within sentences, the sequence of words to use
Use analogies
Be surprising
Make it interesting
Summary of Chapter 2

Chapter 3: Revising

About Chapter 3
Improve by passes
Enlist reviewers
Improve by drafts
Check signposting
Readability indexes
Summary of Chapter 3

PART 2: SPECIAL TECHNIQUES

Chapter 4: Instructions

About Chapter 4
Sentence structure and style
Sequencing
Case, numbering and title
Testing
Summary of Chapter 4

Document Log for ....Informative Writing................. 11 of 12

The Document Plan *(continued)*

Bibliography

This isn't a bibliography in the formal sense of a systematic list of books on subjects related to this book. It's simply a short list of books that might complement your reading of this book. The first four are classics of their kinds.

The Elements of Style
by William I. Strunk and E.B.White.
Strunk's original version first published privately in 1912 in the USA.
Current version published in the USA by Collier Macmillan, and distributed in the UK by International Book Distributers Ltd.
ISBN 0024182001. £4.95.

Language in Thought and Action
by S.I.Hayakawa.
First published in 1939 in the USA.
Last published in the UK by Allen and Unwin. Currently out of print. Libraries might have it. ISBN 0044000251.

Usage and Abusage by Eric Partridge
First published in 1947 in the UK .
Currently published in the UK by Penguin Books. ISBN 0140510249. £5.99.

The Complete Plain Words
by Sir Ernest Gowers.
First published (under that title) in 1954 in the UK by HMSO.
Currently published in the UK by Penguin
ISBN 0140511997. £6.99.

Problem Solving Strategies for Writing by Linda Flowers.
First published in 1985 in the USA.
Currently published in the USA by College Publishers.
ISBN 0155001701. £14.95.

Write Right! A Desk Drawer Digest of Punctuation, Grammar and Style
by Janet G. Venolia.
First published in the USA in 1979.
Writers' News edition published in the UK in 1992 by David St John Thomas.
ISBN 0946537577.

The Structure of English: A Handbook of English Grammar
by Michael Newby.
First published in 1987 in the UK by Cambridge University Press, the current publishers. ISBN 0521349966. £4.25.

Effective Writing: Improving Scientific and Technical Communication
by Christopher Turk and John Kirkman.
First published in 1982 in the UK by E. and F. Spon, the current publishers.
ISBN 0419146601. £11.50.

Good Style: Writing for Science and Technology by John Kirkman.
Published in 1992 in the UK by Spon.
ISBN 0419171908. £11.50.

Full Marks: Advice on Punctuation for Scientific and Technical Writing
by John Kirkman.
Published in 1993 in the UK by Ramsbury Books. ISBN 0952176203. £5.95.

Index